CLUTTER-FREE HOME

HOW TO DECLUTTER, ORGANIZE AND CLEAN YOUR HOUSE IN 15 MINUTES A DAY

SOPHIE IRVINE

CONTENTS

INTRODUCTION

Clutter.

Some people believe it's a part of life. But others know that there is usually more clutter than what's needed. If you feel bogged down by all the clutter in your home and want to make your space better, like something out of an Instagram post, then you're in the right place.

In this book, we'll teach you how to confront the clutter, take care of it, and create a cleaner home than ever before.

However, how do you do it? How can you declutter your space, and keep it decluttered no matter what?

Well, the solution is in this book.

In this, you'll get solutions that allow you to break through all these struggles you have, and get the clutter gone for good!

In this book, you'll learn everything that you need to know

about organizing and decluttering your home, especially if you live in a busy home.

No matter how many soccer practices you need to go to, or how many business meetings you have, we'll tell you how to declutter your space, and how to keep everything in order in just 10-15 minutes a day!

Yes, this is a decluttering book for the busy people in all of us, a set of solutions that will tell you immediately how to go about decluttering your space, so you're happy, and you don't feel overwhelmed by everything in your home.

The Problem

Being able to keep a space clean is very hard. I personally understand the struggle of keeping a space clean and making it stay clean. It's hard, and if you don't have ample time, spending your free days cleaning sounds awful.

But there is a solution to this, and I'll tell you how.

The Solution

The solution to this is simple: a little bit of cleaning each day goes a long way, and in this book, I'll tell you about the small steps you need to take to clean your space, but also how to do it, so you're not spending your days just cleaning.

Cleaning is boring, and decluttering can be overwhelming, but I'll tell you exactly what it is that you need to do, and everything that you should do to keep your space clean, and beautiful. When it comes to cleaning your home, it is possible to make the space clean and usable, no matter what.

My Story

I used to be like you. I worked a full-time job, and I have kids. That alone makes it a nightmare to clean. Every chance I had to clean, I wouldn't do it, because obviously, who wants to spend their days cleaning? I sure don't, and I'm sure you don't want to either.

But, when I learned that it's possible to declutter your home, make it look like something out of a Pinterest post, I grew excited. I decided to try it, and boy was I happy with the results.

I tried all of these different decluttering techniques, working from the easiest over to the hardest ones. I learned how to properly get rid of all the clutter in my home, and also, how to clean it so I felt happy with the results.

This is something everyone can get on board with. For most of us, it's obviously a struggle, and it can be hard for you to start. Trust me, when I sat down and started the decluttering process, I thought I was going to have a heart attack trying to get everything organized. But I learned how to do this effectively, and how to easily create a better home not just for myself, but for my family too.

If you're someone who doesn't like to clean, who would rather sit around than clean your home, I get that. But, do you want to spend your time in a space that's filled with clutter?

Trust me, you don't want to be one of those people on Hoarders, that's for sure. While I'm sure it's not that bad if you keep putting it off, it's just going to make you feel terrible, and you won't want to do anything about it.

The hardest part is starting. I learned when I first did this, starting on this path was hard for me, simply because it required me to face my fears, to actually do something about all the clutter in my home.

I had to sit there and be realistic, understand that some stuff was better off tossed, and I also learned that it isn't bad to throw away things you don't need.

I had to get through this hurdle before I even had a chance to do something about it, and I encourage you as a person to sit down, and realistically look at what you need, what you don't need, and to toss away the stuff that isn't worth it.

Because here's the reality of it: not everything needs to be kept. There are things better off left on the side or donated to another person. Some people can benefit from your stuff.

And there are things that are better left tossed in the garbage. We'll go over as well why people hold onto these material objects so much, and how to overcome your fear of keeping objects, so you're able to, with all of these as well, understand and do something about this. For most of us, when we start to learn and understand why we keep the items that we do, we'll be happier and much better off.

For many of us, learning how to better ourselves, and to create a space that we can use is vital. I do think it's time that you stop sitting around and avoiding it and start doing something about it.

Start Decluttering Today!

If you're stuck on how to start decluttering, then look no further. I'll help you with tips and tricks on how to declutter, and how to start doing it today, so you can have a cleaner tomorrow!

PART 1: DECLUTTERING

CHAPTER 1: ALL ABOUT DECLUTTERING

First, let's talk about decluttering. Before you can organize your space, you must declutter it. Here, we'll talk about decluttering, and the mindset for decluttering.

So What Is It?

When you declutter your home, you're removing all of the items that you feel won't necessarily benefit you if you keep them around. For example, stuff that either has a higher cost than benefit, whether it's financial or time-waster or is just taking up extra space in your home.

For example, let's say you have five different winter coats. You live in a space where it gets to the point where you need to wear a winter coat only like two weeks out of the year. Do you need to have five different winter coats? Course not! That means that it's just taking up needless space in your home. By being there, it really isn't benefiting you.

This is basically getting rid of anything that isn't really benefiting your home, making you a lot happier, and you can enjoy life so much more.

But Isn't That Just Minimalism?

Nope. Minimalism and decluttering are two very different things. With minimalism, you are getting rid of anything that is in excess, and in general, downsizing your home immensely.

So, even if you needed the five different winter coats, you still would keep one, because you're literally keeping just the bare minimum.

The idea behind minimalism is to just keep the minimal, and in general, is getting rid of almost everything. Minimalism is good if you really want to get rid of everything, but it's the more extreme form of this.

Decluttering is just getting rid of things that aren't going to benefit you. It might not be items that don't "spark joy", but instead, it's items that you simply feel are better off given to others than sitting around in your home like a bump on the log.

Like for example, if you don't read books in paperback form, do you need a whole library of books? Or would they be better at a used bookstore, where you might get some cash for them, or if they can't take them, you give them to Goodwill so someone else can use them? That's the idea of decluttering.

It's basically taking all the stuff that you personally feel isn't necessary, and giving them to someone else. Minimalism is a more extreme form of this, and unless you feel like just torching everything you currently have, I suggest keeping the mindset of decluttering more than anything else.

The Best Mindset for Decluttering?

There are some times when you feel like you need to have the mindset of getting rid of everything when you declutter.

However, that isn't the case.

Decluttering isn't just tossing everything you feel is "garbage" and getting rid of it all. It's about being selective in what you choose to get rid of.

Decluttering helps teach you what is important to you, and lets you become more selective of what you keep around. You are choosing what will benefit you, and also what you'll actually use.

Utilization is a big part of this. Look at everything that you keep around, and from there, you can choose what works for you. If you don't think you're going to use something, then go ahead and toss it.

This is a hoarder mentality for some of us to possess. The reason being, that if we're so used to keeping everything, tossing it can be hard.

But, if decluttering is hard for you, you need to focus on whether or not it's really that important. Sure, that dress is nice, but when's the last time you wore it? When do you think you're going to wear it again? If you can't really figure out the answer to that, then that's the problem here. If you can't, then you should toss it.

This is something most people don't realize is a big part of it. For most of us, the idea of tossing stuff we don't need isn't all that hard. But there is sentimentality that goes along with it. Sometimes, you might feel like getting rid of stuff you're not using is bad.

It's not. It clears out your space and helps you figure out what you really want from your decluttered home.

Helps You With Understanding Tastes

One mindset (that is great for those who are really struggling with decluttered homes) is understanding your personal tastes. Personal tastes change. What you liked a year ago might be different now. This is especially true with clothes, or even accessories and collectibles.

If you notice you're still collecting old things that you don't even like, one of the mentalities that you should have when decluttering is to understand that things change. You're allowed to have a different mindset and a different taste for everything that you do. If you feel like you're really not going to benefit from this, then you should definitely just get rid of it.

There are many different benefits to decluttering, and understanding that will help to get the space in order.

Less Stuff, More Space

The biggest benefit of decluttering is the amount of space this gives you. Do you feel like you're grappling with having too much stuff? That's a sign you've got to declutter your space.

If you're so cluttered that you feel obstructed in your path in any way that's hazardous and irritating, you should declutter it.

But it isn't just a physical distraction, but also mental distractions. Do you sometimes look at spaces and feel very distracted by the space, simply because there is so much going on? That's the clutter that's there. You should keep yourself more disciplined and less distracted by decluttering. Sometimes, adopting the mindset of this gives you more space, and less desire to be distracted. It is one of the main reasons to adopt a decluttering mindset. You won't feel as pressured about cleaning, or feel as bad that you haven't, and essentially, you're putting a better foot forward, and you're not bogged down by your stuff.

Decluttering your space is very hard, and it can be a nightmare to do. But, if you know how to do it, then you'll be happier, and understanding what it is exactly, and why you should do it, along with the appropriate mindset for it, will help as well.

CHAPTER 2: THE PERFECT MOMENT TO START DECLUTTERING

So what is the perfect time to start decluttering? The obvious answer is right now, but is there a better time than right now to start decluttering? Well, let's talk about how to start decluttering, and how to avoid the declutter paralysis that many individuals go through.

Spring has Sprung!

Spring is probably the best time for decluttering. That's because it's in between both the hot season and the colder seasons. You've just got done with all the holidays, so you probably have a better idea of what was used and what wasn't used during the holiday season. Another part of that is the clothing you have too.

During the spring, you can accurately look at exactly what jackets you wore during the winter, what excess items you never even touched, and various items that you feel just won't be used. You can also use this as a way to forecast your style for summer. For example, you can realistically look at your collection of summer dresses, and from there, you can decide whether or not it's needed.

Many people like to do this too because of the changing weather. Gone are the days of you sitting inside your home all the time, but instead you're getting out, enjoying the weather, and everything that's going on. It usually means it's nicer to stay outside, and much nicer for you weather-wise too. So, if you need to declutter your outdoor space, this is when to do it.

You can also look at various toys and other items your family has, and toss them away as well. You can look at everything and decide whether or not it will benefit you this coming year, whether it will help you relax, whether it will provide meaningful entertainment if you don't think it can, then there you go. It's not worth it.

But Shouldn't You Do It Now?

Yes, now is the ideal time. If you can, you'll probably want to start right away, but you have to feel that it's genuinely for you, that you will continue with this.

Look at your schedule and figure out whether or not it's possible to declutter during this time. Sometimes, the warmer months are a little easier for decluttering, since you'll have the drive to start, and you'll want to get going.

It also depends on your biological calendar as well. Are you the type who is more productive during the winter months rather than the summer? Then maybe decluttering in these months works for you! But you also run into the hurdle of Christmas and holidays, where you tend to get items, and it's hard to fully break away from that.

Nevertheless, you can start right now, and I encourage you to start as early as you can. But, understand it can be hard for some of us, but worth it at the end of the day if we can overcome these hurdles.

Decluttering Paralysis

This happens when you're trying to start, but you feel almost stuck or guilty because you don't want to get rid of it.

There are a couple of ways to handle it. If you notice that it's happening, you should consider the two questions that are below:

First, ask why you're trying to declutter. What the heck is your reason to declutter? Will it make you feel less stressed? Will you invite more people over and feel less ashamed if you have a decluttered home? Sometimes, when we start, we stop, because we don't know why.

Maybe your motivation is the Pinterest blogs you see with all the pretty homes put neatly together. If that's the case, then continue with that energy. Understanding why decluttering is important to you as a person will help with this. If you notice you're struggling to let go of stuff, you need to sit down and understand that as well.

The idea of letting go is hard. This is something we'll touch upon in a later chapter, but if you do notice a paralysis in certain places you're working to declutter, figure out the why behind it? Are you worried people won't take it? Do you think you're going to feel bad if you keep it? That is a valid thing, but you need to sit down, and understand why you're stressed out about keeping it, and how to get over that stress when you declutter the home.

Holding onto clutter will keep you from getting past the struggles of a cluttered home. You'll be shocked at how easy it is to overcome the struggles of clutter if you know what you're doing and make the changes.

You'll also feel more inspired. If you feel paralyzed in the clutter too, work on spaces that are small, and you can picture how you want the space to look when you finish decluttering and organizing, and figure out how this will make you feel. You'll notice you're much more peaceful, and less overwhelmed if you're working in a home that's less cluttered.

So, when is the best time to declutter your home? That answer is ultimately up to you. Figure out for yourself the best time to do this, and the best course of action to take. Understanding and mastering this will help prevent the paralysis and make your life so much easier for you as well.

Take the time to understand what's holding you back.

CHAPTER 3: DECLUTTERING TIPS, TRICKS, AND HACKS

Now that we've mentioned what it takes to start, let's talk about some of the hacks to make it possible for you to do it. Decluttering your home does take a little bit of time, dedication, and understanding to really do it right.

Start with One Bag of Clothing

First, start with one bag of clothing that you don't wear anymore, for one particular reason. Pick one part of your closet, and look at every item that's in there. Think about whether or not it fits. If it doesn't, then there you go, toss it. If you don't like the style of it, there you go, get rid of it again, or if you don't see yourself wearing it again, then put it in the bag. Fill it up, put it in your trunk, and then drop it off at a donation center next time you're by one. The best way to approach this is to take one place at a time and look at all the clothes you don't wear. As you do it, you'll realize that you'll have more pace, and it's much more suitable than letting it sit there too.

Paper Spots

Paper is one of the most popular sources of clutter. Think about all the papers you get from bills, general mail pieces, coupons, or whatever. If you notice that you're getting a lot of excess paper, you probably put them in so many places. You probably have them on the table, on the counter, in a drawer, on top of a dresser, and pretty much anywhere that isn't one singular spot. If you're someone that keeps losing papers, especially school papers, literally just put it all in one place. Designate one spot for this, and once a week, go through and figure out if you need them. Those expired coupons don't need to be held onto, and you'll realize that, once you get rid of things, life gets a little easier.

Create the Declutter Zones

Declutter zones are essentially the space that you determine will never have clutter, whether it be a kitchen counter, a table, or even just an area around the couch. The idea behind this is simple: everything that's there will never be clutter you don't use. You should always keep this there and just put it away each time. Once you start to do this, expand this until it becomes the entire house. But you should keep everything simple in your space. Even just using one space to confront the declutter, and then move from this will help immensely.

Clean One Surface at a Time

One mistake I see so many people make is they will go and

take on their entire home without realizing that if they do it all at once, they're going to get overwhelmed. What you do is pick one surface.

Personally, I like to start with the counters. This is great because it takes away the clutter from the flat spaces. For example, let's take the kitchen counter. Only keep the necessary appliances on there, and maybe one decorative candle. You should from there look at every single appliance that you have.

If you're not using your waffle maker frequently, then why is it on there? If you're not making blended smoothies, then get rid of it, whether it be storing it on a shelf or even just donating to goodwill. What you need to figure out is how to create a way for you to have spaces that aren't filled with items.

This can even work on non-kitchen surfaces. You don't need to have a stack of magazines on your coffee table, instead, maybe keep one there for decoration, and that's it.

You can do this with shelves too. Whether it's a shelf in a closet, bookshelf, or whatever, you just pick one shelf and work with it. Don't do the whole bookshelf in one moment either, but take literally one shelf, and then clear off any unnecessary items, so it looks clutter-free and neat.

Start Visualizing

When you are decluttering, think about all those rooms that you see and what you want them to look like. Which pieces of furniture do you want? What doesn't belong here but has gravitated towards this spot? What other flat surfaces do you want to clean up? If you start with each little space, choosing one at a time, and going from there, you figure out the essentials, and from this point, get rid of the rest of it.

The visualization helps you with putting an idea out there, and from there, you'll start to understand just what you need in order to help declutter your home.

The 30 Day List

The 30-day list is a simple solution for those of us who get tempted to buy new things as soon as we start decluttering.

You're probably guilty of this. You've spent all that time decluttering, and now, you want to buy a bunch of stuff. Maybe a "treat yourself" gift of a MacBook air or more books for the shelf. The best thing to do is create a 30-day list. Every time you want to buy a thing that isn't totally necessary, what you do is throw it on the list. From there, you keep it there, and if it's been on the list for 30 days, buy it.

However, if you don't want to buy it anymore, scratch it off the list. This is a crazy thing that totally works because you'll notice over time that the urge to buy items will start to go away, and you'll save yourself both money and space. This is super effective and wonderful for those of us who are guilty of impulse buys.

Simple Folder Sand Filing

Finally, start to file and create folders for everything. These pile up high, and you should create some folders with different labels on them, for both the simple paperwork and the major bills. Have everything in one specific spot, and when the system is there, you just file this easily. It doesn't have to be perfect, so if you have extra labels there, put them on, and then there you go.

You should also set up a simple filing system as well, and from here, take a handful and work with them. Make very quick decisions and don't ruminate on that one. Once the system is in place, you file as needed, and make a note of the actions you need to. Don't put anything back into the pile, but work with it. If you can't do anything with it, and if you don't think it's a necessary piece of paper, simply toss it.

Hanging About

If you have clothes that you're never wearing, what you should do is, every time you wear something, change the side of the hanger. For example, have them all hang with the edge of it sitting out, and from there, when used, you flip it. Continue to do that, and after a year, if you realize you never touched some of the dresses you have, you should from there get rid of them.

If they are seasonable clothes, put them in a box, and if you notice that you never touched the box, then just get rid of them period.

These hacks are the best way to go about decluttering the space. I get that decluttering is hard, it's definitely not a simple thing for any of us, but with the proper care, and the right steps, it's possible.

CHAPTER 4: OVERCOMING THE GUILT OF DECLUTTERING IN JUST A FEW MINUTES

It happens to the best of us. We find items that we have sentimental attachment towards, and we feel bad for tossing them. This is something that happens to many of us more often than we think, but these emotions won't go away. Here, we'll discuss the best way to cope with this and how to deal with the emotions at hand.

Why Does It Happen?

Decluttering guilt happens because, when you start to declutter, you come to the realization that you have a lot of unnecessary stuff.

You start to wonder whether you should hold onto it for the simple reason, you might use it again in the future.

This type of guilt happens because people feel bad for getting rid of things. This especially happens if you have a lot of perfectly cleaned and useful things.

Sure they might be useful to someone else, but when's the last time you used them.

This guilt does tie into the decluttering paralysis that occurs when you start cleaning. You feel guilty for doing this, even though the reality is, you're never going to use it.

The guilt can stop you from decluttering some spaces, and you might not be motivated to get rid of it.

What's the easiest way to rectify this situation then? Well, I know what I did, and I'll tell you how to do it.

How to Handle Decluttering Guilt

The best way to do it is to have the motivation to declutter. Why are you doing it? Look at why decluttering this will benefit you, and if you need to, stop and list out the benefits of decluttering, and how to handle it.

When you declutter, keep that motivation, and keep that energy going. It will handle the issues that come up when you declutter and help you feel less guilty.

When you do feel guilty about abandoning items, look at why that is? Is it because you fear getting rid of items? Do you think there might be a reason for keeping it that's eating away at you? Do you feel bothered when you get rid of items? Look at the exact science behind why you feel guilty exactly, and why it is eating away at you. Once you do that, you'll start to realize that it's just the past making you feel guilty.

If it's something that you bought with someone that has

emotional ties to it, sit there and realistically look at whether or not that will benefit you, and whether or not you should even keep it. As well, think about whether or not you're going to use this.

I had this issue with a blender I got. It was a gift from my parents for my wedding, and that, along with many of the other household items had sentimental value to me, even though they were just material things. I looked at this, and I thought to myself whether or not this is better kept or tossed. I realized the reason I felt guilty about this wasn't that I was afraid to toss it, but I felt guilty getting rid of items my parents had given to me.

But, when I looked at how much I'd use it, or even if it was worth keeping around, I started to realize it's better to toss things you don't need, and better to get rid of them.

The guilt of decluttering is a real thing, and it's a frustrating thing to deal with, mostly because people don't realize that holding onto these items does make you feel almost bad. But, if you understand why you feel bad, and understand that feeling guilty will only hang around if you don't get rid of it, it can help with the hurdles you're going over, and the struggles of decluttering.

CHAPTER 5: THE ROOM-BY-ROOM GUIDE TO DECLUTTERING

In this chapter, we'll highlight the exact strategies you need to take in order to declutter the space room-by-room, and how to handle every single room.

Living Room

First, let's talk about the living room. The best way to handle this is simple:

• Begin with the counters, clearing off the clutter there.

• Look at the couch, and put away all items that don't belong there.

• Fold blankets, and any that are old and ratty, you toss.

• Look at gaming systems, and get rid of any clutter that's there, especially cables.

• Clean off your entertainment system of anything that doesn't belong there, or anything you won't use.

• If you have DVDs or CDs that you don't think you're going to use, toss them.

• If there are any knick knacks that don't belong there, get rid of them right away.

• Clear off any furniture that has stuff that you don't need there.

• If you have excess furniture, consider tossing it or getting rid of it.

• Clear off one shelf at a time, and make sure that they're neatly organized.

• If you have bookshelves, clear off each shelf of any books that aren't necessary.

Bedrooms

Bedrooms depend a lot on how you want them to look. Some people like a simple style for their bedrooms, others like it when you have more items around. Here, we'll talk about how to clear up bedrooms of clutter.

• Start with the closets, first and foremost going in, and finding all of the items you haven't worn in the last year. Try them on, and if you don't like how they fit, or they're too big or too small, you toss them.

• Look at any extra items sitting in your drawers. If they don't fit there, toss them or put them in the rightful place.

• Look at socks and undergarments. Lots of us keep the old raggedy underwear and hosiery, so it's better if you just toss anything with holes in it.

• Look at the different types of clothes you wear, especially jackets and coats. If you don't see yourself wearing them, then toss them.

• For the bed, if you have too many pillows and excess things, get rid of them.

• For drawers and vanities, get rid of anything that's too much on the counters, and either clear them off by putting them in their rightful place or toss them.

Kitchen

The kitchen can be hard to declutter quickly, but here, we'll highlight some of the best decluttering tasks for the kitchen:

• Take the stuff you don't use off the countertops.

• Take a small shelf in the fridge, look at the items, and if you see anything you don't use, or can't eat, or it's expired, just toss it. Take one shelf at a time.

• For the kitchen table, keep it uncluttered as much as you can, finding homes for everything on there.

• For the cabinets, grab anything that's not needed, and just give it away or toss it.

• If you have lots of cups, look for any broken ones and toss those as needed.

• On the floor, try to keep everything as neat as possible.

• For the pantry, keep items off the floor, and if you notice something hasn't been touched food-wise in over a month, get rid of it.

Bathrooms

Decluttering the bathroom is quite easy, and here, we'll high-light the top things you've got to worry about when you're cleaning the bathroom:

• Clean the area under the sink, getting organizers and getting rid of any beauty products you don't use.

• If you have makeup that's over a year old, toss it.

• If you have beauty products that you don't use, toss them.

• Look at the medicine cabinet, and if you have old prescriptions, toss these bad boys.

• Look at any hair products, and if you know you and the family don't use them, either toss or give them away to someone who does.

• Get rid of any clutter around the toilet, sink, and counters. Keep it minimal.

• If you have a lot of toothbrushes or toothpaste, if they aren't bad or look grungy, store them in a spot to use, and get rid of them if they're gross.

• If you have empty shampoo and soap bottles or dispensers, either fill them up or toss them.

Home Office

With the home office, this one might take a little bit longer, simply because of all the stuff you might have that you don't know what to do with. But here are a few tips for decluttering this area easily:

• Handle all the papers and put them in one area.

• Sort all the papers, and never leave any of them unread.

• Clear off the countertop of the office for only the essentials like a laptop, notepad with a plan, and so on.

• If you have drawers, tackle one drawer at a time, and get rid of any papers stashed there, or any stuff that isn't necessary.

• If you have any papers or items on your office furniture such as chairs and cushions, take them and put them in the rightful place.

• Look at the bookshelf, and see if there are items that you don't need. If there are, simply get rid of them.

• Do a sweep of your office every day, looking for any excess clutter, but not spending much time on the space.

Craft Room

The craft room and playrooms tend to be messier than others, but here, we'll highlight some of the best ways to declutter this space, so it's meaningful

• If your child has outgrown the toys that they have, or they haven't touched them in a bit, put them in a box to donate, unless you have another kid who might grow into some of them.

• Get any old crayons or other items and put them all neatly in a container to use.

• If you have craft items, put them in an organizer or a shelf, and neatly go through them, see if you'll use any of it.

• If you have lots of excess sewing scraps, if you know you can't use a scrap, then toss it. If you know you won't be making anything with it, then toss that as well.

• If you have a messy counter for crafting, get rid of anything that you don't need.

• Put any crafting tools in one specific area, and if any are broken, then get rid of them.

• If you're using foam crafts, create one specific space for all the film, and foam there, put it all in one singular location.

Any Clothes

Clothes are harder, but there are a few ways to really clean up a clothing space, and here, we'll talk about that:

• If you have any clothes just sitting about, get them to the right space.

• If an article of clothing has holes in it, get rid of it.

• Take one drawer, one closet, one wardrobe at a time: don't try to organize all the spaces at once.

• If you notice you have items you can't remember you last wore, you should toss them.

• If nothing else, try the hanger technique.

• If you have socks without mates and haven't found the mates, get rid of the socks.

• If you can't think of a place to wear the items, then don't keep the item, just toss it.

Storage

Finally, we have storage, which is hard because you run into the "well maybe I'll use that" concept when looking through it. But here we'll highlight some decluttering you can do for a storage space, whether it's an attic or otherwise:

• If you haven't touched the item in the last five years, then toss it.

• If you can't think of a use for this item, then toss it.

• If you have seasonal clothes up there, go through it, and if you have multiples of a seasonal item you don't need, just toss it.

• If you have old decorative items that you keep putting off of tossing, then it's better to toss them.

• The only thing that might just be worthless or mostly sentimental that you keep are family heirlooms, but keep them off to the side so they're not mixed in.

• If you have some boxes with house figurines or the like, keep them all in one box, that way it takes up less space.

• Don't get hung up on keeping things you don't need when decluttering this space.

Storage is probably harder than the other spaces, since most of the time the intent of storage items is to store them, but this is a good place to declutter.

Don't spend a lot of time on any of these locations, but instead, be aware of everything you're tossing, so you're able to, with this as well, toss all the items you don't need.

CHAPTER 6: SELL, DONATE, OR TRASH — WHAT DO YOU DO WITH IT?

This is something most people run into later on. They don't know whether they'll benefit by selling, donating, or trashing the items. If you're at a loss for what to do with this, then you should take some time to read this chapter and understand where to go with it.

When to Sell

The best time to sell is if the item is in near-perfect condition, but you don't have a use for it.

Some of us have clutter in the form of dresses with tags, items still in-boxes that we never opened, and just items that we kept around but never got around to doing anything with them.

These types of items are perfect for selling.

Now, you may wonder where you're supposed to sell these

things. The best bet is to sell them in a place where people will more likely buy them . If you have time for a yard sale or want to collaborate with others on one giant yard sale, then great. Sometimes, flea markets, if you have any time to spend at these, might be good, or if you have family willing to help.

If you're okay with holding onto these for a bit, then throw it on eBay or Amazon. If you have a popular product, the supply and demand might be limited on it, so you could sell it for a pretty penny in response.

Selling is best when you have the item in place, but you don't need it, and you think it's better left with someone else.

When to Donate

The best time to donate items is if they are items that you don't feel like you're going to sell, or you don't have the time and desire to sell these items.

The best items to sell are usually the ones in near-mint condition, but if you have old clothing, stuff in older styles or just items that you don't think there's a demand for, donating is the best way to do it.

The best part about donating is it helps others. Goodwill, for example, has a very simple donation system. You don't even need to use goodwill to do this. There are different donation centers and thrift stores to choose, and if you want to use this means to donate, then, by all means, go for it.

For most of us, donating is an easier route. If you don't have the time to sell it on a site or have a garage sale, and if it's older items that you feel people don't want or just random stuff that you think might be better just donated, then this is the best plan for you. Plus, if you're helping charities, it's definitely not a bad thing.

When to Trash It!

Trashing is probably the last course of action you should take with your items.

If you can't donate it, then you trash it.

Trashed items are usually things that don't benefit anyone because they're old, such as in the case of old, rotten food, or raggedy undergarments and socks. Anything with holes in it is better off just trashed.

The thing about trashing, however, is if you can give it to someone else, that's better. I'm talking more from an environmental standpoint. For most of us, when we just trash it, it's going into a landfill, and some things aren't properly broken down.

If you can recycle it somehow, that's the better option. Old clothes make great cleaning rags.

But, if you're not sure, take it to the charity to donate. Sometimes, they'll take some things you were otherwise going to trash. For food pantries, if you have some food that hasn't gone bad, then you can donate it. But, if the expiration date is long gone, then you're going to have to trash it, no matter how useful it might be.

The "Maybe" Box

There is also the maybe box. This is something you should have on hand when you're going through stuff, and if it's something that you're not sure about whether to keep, trash, or donate, this is where you keep it. Sometimes, you have stuff that you don't use a lot, but you might need it eventually. If it gives you that thought that getting rid of it may not benefit you, this is where the maybe box comes in. This is a box that's kind of hidden so that you're not totally thinking about it all the time. The concept behind this is to see if you actually use this.

Now, when you're not organizing your space and using it, if you think about this item, you should go over and grab it. From there, put a date on the box of six months from now. Six months later, look in the box, and pull out everything that's in there.

See if there is anything that you don't need from this. If you find some item that you know you'll use, maybe like a snow-blower or a leaf blower during certain seasons, then keep it. Usually though, you'll then dump the whole box, because you never really needed it, and it's a good idea to have this around. From there, you can donate, sell, or trash it.

For most of the items that you have, donation is the way to go. That's because, when you donate the item, someone else is going to get good use out of this. This also helps with the guilt you feel when you're getting rid of items. Sometimes, just thinking of the fact that someone else might benefit from this is enough to help you get rid of it. Plus, you're thinking about others, which is a good thing.

This is a big part of decluttering, and hopefully, you now have an idea of where to put all of the items that are there.

CHAPTER 7: KISS STRATEGY — HOW 10 MINUTES A DAY KEEPS THE CLUTTER AWAY!

This is an important part, and it's super simple to do. Keeping it simple is the way you declutter, and it can help make the whole process easier to take care of.

The reason why you have clutter is probably because you were a little lazy with putting stuff away. Sometimes you just leave something there and think "I'll do it later", but you never do it later.

Sometimes, we're all too busy with our lives, and if you work a job, chances are you don't want to sit around and worry about the nuances of how cluttered your house is. Most of us don't want to spend the time or the extra steps putting mail into the shredder or sorter, instead, we leave it lying on the counter.

We'll do this with everything. If we have a jacket we wore but don't need it now, we're more inclined to throw it on the floor or the couch, rather than put it away. Sometimes it might be because we're just hurrying from one part of the room to the next part, rather than actually looking at what we're doing and being mindful.

The idea behind decluttering is to get rid of the stuff you don't need, and from there, you put the rest in its rightful place. That's all it is, and that's how it should be.

While you might have some really deep and thoughtful process on decluttering, the best way to do it is KISS—Keep it Simple, Stupid.

This isn't an attempt to make you feel bad or belittle you, but instead, understand it doesn't take much to clean up your home.

For many of us, we think it takes forever, but it doesn't. Not when you've already put everything in place and work to clean it up.

Seriously, Keep It Simple

If nothing else, be simple with this. You can create small reminders on the various tasks, such as a sign that says, "Don't put clutter here!" and then tape this in the spot where people tend to leave cutter. Even just posting it on the fridge might be a good, gentle reminder.

Some people think they need to put together some complex color-coordinated system of keeping clutter away. That's fine and dandy if you want to go through those motions, but here's the thing: keeping it simple is the way to go.

If you do these complex systems, it won't create a habit. The goal here is a habit because that will, in turn, help you keep the space properly cleaned. If you don't form a habit, then you're going to have a rough time.

I like to figure out the easiest ways to do it. You know what they say: if you do it the laziest way, it requires the least work.

I'm not saying don't ever put your stuff away, but put it all in a place where, if possible, there is no clutter.

Just Put Your Stuff Where It Belongs!

If nothing else, start putting stuff where it belongs. This is part of the simple solution to declutter and maintain an orderly home.

What this means is, instead of just throwing your coats, backpacks, or whatever all around like they're just some toy, take everything, and mindfully put it back where it came from.

I don't care if it is somewhere that you use a lot, or a place you rarely touch; just put it back where it belongs. Having a home for the items you need is so important that you'd be surprised at how effective it is to follow this.

Sometimes the Easiest Systems Work the Best

There are those of us who think that we need to make some methodical plan and deep schedule where we need to follow everything to the letter, and focus only on doing that.

No, you don't have to. Seriously, keep it simple, stupid.

One of the biggest mistakes you can make with decluttering your home is that you don't realize that if you try to use the hard and complicated systems, you just get very overwhelmed. What you need to do is put together the system that will help you out, and one that you'll keep.

The way to do it is pretty simple: if you have a room, pick a spot, declutter it, and don't move forward till that's finished. Do not pass go, do not collect 200. This keeps you focused, and if you keep it simple, it'll make things easy.

Start with One Thing at a Time

I'm sure you probably have a bunch of areas that need decluttering, but the easiest way to keep this simple is to just start with one area, and go from there. This is the easiest way to do it, simply because if you do this any other way, you're going to get overwhelmed, and you're not going to be happy.

What I like to do is work in one space, and then when I'm fully done with that, I work on another space. You might not even fully declutter one space in a day, and that's okay!

The best thing to remember about all of this is that if you declutter it in this fashion, it'll be easier on you as well.

Building your own personal plan to declutter it in just one step at a time is essential, and very important because otherwise, you'll get overwhelmed, and unhappy.

The idea of taking this a step at a time might seem trite and boring to most people, and you might feel like you're on this forever, but you don't have to be.

Your mindset is the other thing you also need to keep simple.

A Simple Mindset for a Simple Job

One part of KISS you have to understand is that while yes, it's physical, it's also a mental thing too. Don't sit there and try to get rid of stuff and think of all of the reasons to keep a dress you haven't worn at all in the last three years, just ask yourself if you've worn it, and if you can't say yes, then toss it.

"But what about"—If you don't see yourself using this or can't think of a reason to keep it, then toss it to the side.

This is a big one. The problem with most of us is we are thinking people. We could come up with a thousand reasons to keep that creepy collector's item that's stowed away in the back, but even you don't want to look at it, but that doesn't mean you have to do that.

The biggest thing to remember is that you need to keep a simple mentality along with a simple physical activity from it too. If you think you won't use it, then toss it. If you don't have an exact use or reason for this, then get rid of it. If you don't think you'll actually have a purpose for this, then why are you keeping this stuff around?

One part of setting and forgetting that we often forget about, and one of the biggest things to remember when cleaning up your space, is that you have the power to decide the fate of all of your items, no matter how big or how small they are. If you don't think you need it, you have to learn to let go. And some-times the quick and dirty way of deciding this is more valuable than sitting here ruminating on why you should keep this thing you haven't touched in months.

The concept of a simple mindset for a simple job is something we need to adopt. If you do this in a way that's simple, you'll get through this faster, and you'll be happier too. This is a big thing to remember, and a big part of decluttering.

Know the Giveaway Items That You Can Toss Right Away

This one is important. If you already know of things that you don't need, then by all means, just toss these bad boys. Get rid of them like a bad apple.

If you have old, rotting food somewhere, get rid of it. If you have clothes that are too spoiled to wear again, then toss them. If you have children's toys, that you know nobody in the house will use, then toss them. This is a big part of decluttering, and you have to remember that one of the biggest parts of decluttering is knowing what you need to toss and what's willing to be kept around.

When you do this, you'll realize that decluttering items for the trash is much easier than you think. People don't realize that this is the beginning of the process, and you have to keep this simple. To do otherwise will defeat the purpose of this, and if you don't take care of this now, it'll just pile up.

That's also a big part of keeping the space clean after decluttering. If that food's old, get that off the counter! If you know, you're not going to wear this again, either sell or donate. You don't need to get into the whys and wherefores of your stuff, just be smart, and start to toss anything that you know won't benefit your life anytime soon. It's good to be honest with yourself on this, but also know that, once it's over, you'll be happier with less stuff.

Keeping it simple is very important, and if you're not keeping it simple when decluttering, then what's the point? Getting out of the complexities of your head so you can throw away items you don't need is important and valuable for you as a person.

PART 2: ORGANIZING

CHAPTER 8: AFTER THE FALLOUT — HOW TO ORGANIZE WHAT'S LEFT

So you've finally gotten rid of all the stuff that you have, and now you're ready to organize. Congrats, and now, you'll learn every single step that's in place to teach you how to organize any part of your home, and how to do it effectively.

Organize Your Home into "Zones"

Zones are essentially how you divide a room. This makes the organizing of a space less overwhelming, and it is a good way to sort other items that you have. If you have a kitchen, for example, you will have specific places for the supplies you need for baking, your cutlery, any staples, and also plates and cups. Having all of this in place is a form of organizing.

Another zone is the linen closet, where you'll have towels, cleaning supplies, linens, basic household needs such as paper towels, and from there, you take stock of where these go, take such items and organize them based on each zone.

Focus on Accessibility

The idea behind this is the more an item is used, the easier it should be to access. What you have to do is to store the items that you use daily towards the front and more towards your eye level. The concept behind that is that if you need it, it's right there and you don't have to spend money purchasing that once again. If you have cupboards, get some of those small pull-out bins for this in order to make it accessible. The tiered shelving with the back visible is a good one too, and that's definitely a good idea for this.

You should also consider the location of where they're going, and try to store these in the area as much as you'll be using them, especially if it's a daily occurrence. Kids' storage areas for their supplies should, of course, be low and easily accessible.

Make it Easy to Look At

The one thing with organization is you need to make it so that you can actually use it, and that it's easy to look at. Sure, a card catalog filing system for everything might seem like a good idea at first, but if it's too organized, it feels almost tedious to keep up with. You should be able to look at it, see what you need, and then take your stuff out, and then put it back where it belongs when you're finished with the job. That's the ultimate goal of this, and what you should be going for as well. Understand that, and you'll understand the concept of organization.

Make it look pretty, but also, know exactly where everything is in its own way, so you're able to, with this as well, put together the easiest shelving system, and process you can put together. Remember, you want to use this, right? Then make sure it can be usable.

Space Optimization

One part of this is to optimize the space for both function and storage. For example, hooks, bars, storage caddies, and those little carriages for projects to help make it work for you. Adding these to the closets on the sidewalls is good.

When you have tiny storage faces, think in a vertical manner, and add additional shelving to the higher up areas for the seasonal items, or those not as frequently used, or even a storage unit that's walled. The big thing to remember is to not be afraid to get creative with this and figure out the multi-use pieces that work for decoration, along with storage too. Figure out your space, how you want to use it, and the best way to apply this as well.

If you do this, you'll be able to use it, and in your own way so that you're happy with the results.

Again, Keep It Simple, Stupid

This is again, simple, and you want to make sure that you keep it in a way that's simple for you to maintain. Keep it simple, and keep it in a way that you actually want to make it so that you're able to use this. You should make sure that you don't make it so that you have to move twenty other items in order to get to one box. That's silly, and you want to make sure that every item you have is accessible with one step.

For example, if you have a certain type of makeup you need then go get it. For items that you need less of, then keep it two steps to get it. The big thing to remember here is you don't want to move a bunch of stuff out of the way to just get one item. For those items that are less frequently used, the two steps rule is the way to go.

The idea is that the easier it is for you to grab it, the more it'll be used. And it'll also make it possible for your family to use it too. It's easier to get your husband to actually put away the dishes or the groceries if it's in a way that's easy for him to do, rather than some convoluted way that only benefits you, right?

Don't Buy Organization Bins at the Beginning

The big thing to remember with this one is that while those organization systems are wonderful to use, limit your purchase of them till after you're done with putting things away. Bins, baskets and the like are great for keeping your items nice and neat, and they're ideal for making everything tidy, but the thing is, you should try to buy all this at the end of the process because you want to enhance the organization, not build it around these items.

Having five storage bins is great, but did you really need those five when a small caddy holding everything would have sufficed? People don't realize this, and then, they end up wondering where all their money went. Well, it's because they were buying the organizational items instead of just organizing.

A lot of people who are trying to organize fast end up

making this mistake, and it's a fatal error. It can end up ruining the entire process, and it can be quite cumbersome to you. So, it's in your best interest to make sure that, if you do use organization products, that's great, but you should also be willing to make sure to use other ways to organize your home as well.

Label It!

If you want to make it easy to use, use labels. People will know where to put things if it's got a nice label on it. Your family will thank you if you take the time to use labels on everything. This is incredibly helpful for trying to get into storage or reach the areas that are difficult to well, reach. If you know where to put something because of a fancy label, this reduces the instance of putting it in a basket that's random and thereby, also reducing the chance of people not putting stuff where it needs to go.

Evaluate and Modify

After you've started to organize, you should look at the space that you have, and see whether or not it can be adequately maintained. Very organized spaces will be easy to maintain with only a few minor additions or changes. If you notice that this space is starting to get cluttered again, look at it, and start to see if you have too much stuff in there. If the items that are difficult to access, require multiple steps, and whether or not things are put back in the right spot or not. This last one is mostly just resolved by being more diligent about where you put your items.

The idea behind this is to tweak everything and get back to the drawing board with all of this and do this with the space.

One thing to remember with decluttering is that it's a process that continuously happens. If you declutter a little, you need to organize a little bit more too. Sometimes you might need to declutter a little bit more, and then purchase a couple of bins for it, and put those away. Sometimes even decluttering to put items properly away is the best option for this too, and you should understand that, with organization, it will make a difference. You need to understand that organizing is a process, and it's something that you should try to work on bettering and mastering over time.

Don't Mass Organize Any Room

The big thing you've got to remember is that you should never declutter an entire space in one fell swoop. Start with a space, and then work from there. For example, start with maybe a cabinet, a shelf, or whatever, and after you've decluttered it, organize this bad boy. This will, in turn, help your home look better, and you won't get as overwhelmed.

You need to understand as well that doing this room by room in a tiny manner is better for those of us that have a busy schedule. After all, who wants to spend hours reorganizing their room?

I don't, and I don't think you want to either.

The best way to do this is to declutter slowly, and declutter and organize based on each space. Sometimes, you'll realize some places are better off with certain items than others, but understanding that you have to figure out the home for all your stuff is just as important too.

For rooms, you should always consider the way you organize each space and any shelving that's there for you to use.

How to Approach a Space

When looking at decluttering, what you need to do is first and foremost, look at each space you have, whether it be a drawer, a cabinet, or whatever. From there, picture how you want the room to look, including each and every different way to organize and make it easier to approach. From here, figure out the process you want to make this work. Then, you do it, and finally, you adjust, label, and put everything back as needed.

It's that easy, but you have to understand that it's definitely not easy for you to do, and sometimes when you organize, you'll realize it's hard to keep things all tidy. But, keep it simple stupid, and understand that, once you've finished a space, move onto the next one.

Now that you know how to organize spaces, you will now learn how to use different organization methods to clean up each room, and organize it effectively.

CHAPTER 9: THE BEST IN-DEPTH GUIDE ON HOW TO ORGANIZE YOUR SPACE

So how do you organize a room in each space? Well, we're about to go through each and every single room and give you the exact tips, tricks, and ideas to help you clean up your space within each room.

Living Room

For the living room, there are a few ways to really keep it nice and tidy, and this section will discuss how you can keep your living rooms very orderly and inviting .

• Put a small, decorative wastebasket in your living room to help keep trash out of there as much as possible.

• Get a small little basket to put the magazines, papers, books, or brochures and make sure that you keep it clutter-free on every surface.

• If you have extra pillows and blankets, get a small basket, fold them up, and nicely put them next to the couch.

• Fluff every pillow at least once a week to help make them look nice and full.

• For entertainment systems, start to get cord organizers to help keep everything tidy around there.

• If you have game systems, neatly wrap the cords and put them into a small little basket to the right of where the consoles are.

• Wrap up all of the wires you have, neatly put a cord organizer on them, and from there, set them on the side. Having a plastic bucket is great for this.

• If you have any small knick knacks, try to reduce them from where the flat surfaces are in your home.

• Put either a small bookcase or a table with some storage bins underneath if you don't have a playroom for kids to sit in and enjoy everything, and you can add rolling toy bins to help keep everything there.

• Add rolling baskets or bins under your coffee table to help store the clutter such as remote controls, drink coasters, or even magazines.

• Keep a separate shelving area for games, and make sure to keep it neatly organized.

• Get an armoire that will house all of your games and systems, and make sure that the surfaces are neatly organized.

• Consider hanging up your photos or even using a digital photo album rather than just throwing them on your coffee table or flat surface, since it will reduce your clutter, or you can keep them on the bookshelf in one location.

• You can also put the blankets and pillows behind the sofa or even the cabinet or bookcase if you feel like that's a better location for these items.

Bedrooms

Your bedrooms are the next location that you should consider looking into. As the closet is such a significant and large area, we'll discuss this later on, here are some organization tips that will help you put your bedroom into a rightful place.

• Consider using the area underneath your bed to store some of the different items that you need, such as gift wrap, linens for the room, or for kids bedrooms some extra books and toys

• Put your artwork on the wall, and don't leave it on the night-stand or dresser, and it will help keep a more streamlined appearance.

• Keep all of your flat surfaces as decluttered as possible, and try to keep a more cohesive look that's organized to your space.

• Consider a rack for your blankets, and install this rack right next to the bed. This is great if you have a lot of throws, quilts, and bedding that you don't really feel like putting away, and it makes turning the bed down easier. Plus, it does ultimately save a lot of floor space.

• Again, get some baskets for your pillows, and try to put them on a basket that's next to the bed. You can also, if you strip your bed down every night, put it all in there and grab it in the morning in order to help make it functional for everyone.

• Keep a night table that is functional with an organizer on that, or also a small dresser and some of the small little knick knacks and a lamp there. Try to make sure it's both functional and clutter-free as well.

• Have a hamper in every bedroom. That way, you won't have to worry about clothes not being washed or strewn all across the floor. You can get one that fits the home, or even just a basic hamper.

• If you dislike how the hamper looks, throw it in your closet. It keeps it out of your hair, and in turn, will help to make the space much easier to work with.

• Make sure every place has a garbage bin, your bedroom included. A small little pail works that you can throw right next to the nightstand is ideal.

You can throw small pieces of trash, tissues, or scraps of paper into there, and it doesn't have to be something big and obnoxious, but rather, something small and functional.

Kitchen

The kitchen is the next disaster zone to tackle, and boy can it be terrible. Here are a few little tips to help you make it so that you can use your kitchen easily and effectively.

• Get rid of some of those plastic containers that are stained, won't fit together correctly, or have cracks. From there, stack by size, and from here use dividers to stash the lids, and then sort it by size for very easy visibility. Try to replace these slowly but surely with glass ones before the end of the year, since it is safer and easier for you to use as well.

• If you have a lot of plastic bags, get a small container, and put it into there. This is a canister that can be covered with cardstock, and from there, decorated to spell bags with letting. Roll your plastic bags into a small circle, and thread the first bag through there and pull it up. If done right, it will then start to move upwards as you grab one, and it beats having an entire cabinet of plastic bags, right?

• Clean out and organize your fridge. You should've already gotten rid of all the bad stuff, but now take some small containers and put these in there. Have everything in a place where it would make sense to be put. You can actually look at the different types of foods and organize it by that, the most frequently used foods near the front, and try to use baking soda to clean your fridge rather than actual cleaners, because you don't want that on your food.

• For the cabinets, try to maximize your cabinet space by putting stemware glasses upside down and look at your dishes, putting the more frequently used items near the bottom since that's, of course, more convenient. Try using the interior shelves too in order to accommodate the other dishes. Consider putting nesting bowls and casserole dishes on the stationary shelves too.

• Get an organizer for your coffee stuff, whether it be the

sugar, cream, or whatever, and then, install small little hangers for your coffee mugs and have them within easy reach. It's simple but wonderful for your space.

• For the utensils, get one of those organizers for this. There are a variety of different types of organizers these days, and the best thing to do is to get one that fits everything, and from there, put your stuff back in. Don't try to just pile things up to wherever, but instead, have it neatly organized so this can be used.

• Water bottles can be stored with an organizer in cabinets, similar to how you store wine bottles. Having the water bottles on their sides does eliminate the chance they might fall and knock stuff over, and plus, you can always just grab and go with these and then move onto the next thing.

• Organize your stuff based on use, and if you have stuff that you use a lot, devote more room to it. If you're going to use it often, leave it out, otherwise, set it inside a drawer. You can even devote parts of your cabinet and counters to baking, putting everything in there so that you can have it all there, and easily attain it.

• Your pantry might already be neatly decluttered, but if you haven't organized it yet, you should consider using a lazy Susan for your species, sauces, and a door organizer for more storage if you need it. Make sure that your pantry is grouped ideally by alphabet, and keep the items you use the most right on hand for best results.

• Add hooks over your oven or stove, and from there, hang all of the utensils that you have on hand. Putting it all there gives you an idea of the areas of everything, and having these on a wood plank right above there keeps everything nicely in place, and you'll be happy to use these as well.

• For appliances, you can have them placed in a cabinet that's vertical, with shelving that you use to pull open. The best way to do this one is to add some labels, and if you have tall appliances, try to put them in smaller spaces, and neatly store them there. Remember to purge appliances that you don't need, selling as necessary.

• Keep stuff for kids pretty low, and if they do have school lunches. Having it together and in a place for them to take at the beginning of the day is essential, and helpful.

Bathrooms

Bathrooms do require a certain level of organizing too. And here we'll highlight the best ways for you to organize your bathrooms so that you can actually find everything.

• If you haven't already, take a built-in shelving space, and put it under your sink. This is valuable storage space people don't need, and oftentimes, this can mean a difference between having room for what you need and what you don't have room for.

• Always have a small little space to keep everything off the counter. Try to keep only a few items there that you use. You should definitely try to make sure it looks nice too.

• Getting a foaming soap pump can enhance the room, and it

doesn't require a lot of soap either to fill this. You can actually label it too with some free labels that you can find online and print out for even more fun.

• The inside of your cabinet doors is just as important as the inner cabinet themselves. You can use this for different hair styling products and the like. These over-the-door organizers are great for face towels and cleaning cloths.

• Get a toothbrush organizer, and try to put it under the cabinet. That way, it's easy to find, but also incredibly out of sight so that it doesn't look bad, and also is easy for you to grab when needed.

• Drawer dividers let you get the most out of your drawers. There are acrylic ones that work especially for the bathroom since it makes these light and airy, and it also lets you add the drawer liner for your own personal touch. Pretty nifty, aren't they?

• Get a caddy for each person in the home. Having a caddy for these items lets them have all of their hygiene products in one place. They can pull out the caddy, use it, and then put it back. That way, everything is there, and they don't forget things. Plus, it's very easy and quick to clean up. You can get small ones, or big ones for this.

• If you don't already have a laundry bin, get one in your home. It doesn't need to be anything big, but having this is also good for any towels, other pieces of clothing that might've not made it to the room, so it helps to make laundry day a little easier on everyone.

• Try considering hanging towels from hooks instead of those towel bars. It's much easier to hang from a hook than a towel bar, it allows them to dry better, and it will definitely be much easier too.

Towel bars are ideal for those who will actually use smaller towels, and this works. Getting a bunch of hooks for each person will help cut down on washing, and also help keep the place nice and clean.

• Finally, use clear acrylic containers and label everything on these containers. Labeling should be your best friend. You can use these on pretty much anything that you're buying or getting, and that will help you with your space.

Home Office

The home office is another place you should always have ideas for organizing, and here, we'll highlight how to organize your home office.

• If you have a lot of cords, get those binder clips, and detangle the cables and USB cords. Clip these to the side of your desk, and then thread the metal part, so it's tangle free.

• The mason jar method is great for office supplies. Hot glue some mason jars together on the sides, and then have them on the desk.

Use them on their sides then and put pens, pencils, staples, and small office supplies in them. Another great one to use in your crafting space as well.

• One way to store some of the items is a jelly jar for storage.

Remove your shelf and place it upside down, and then screw, nail, or put the hot glue lid onto there, and keep the jars onto the shelf. This is a good way to keep things all neatly in place.

• If you don't already have a pegboard over your desk to help with your notes and papers, or even tape and scissors, consider having this in place.

• If you have old shutters, nail these to the wall. You can use this to hold some of the pending and paid bills that you have, or small pieces of paperwork, and you can use the top half as an inbox and the bottom half as an outbox. Little different, hey?

• If you have old shoeboxes, you can pin these together with clips in order to store different papers and books. You can also cover these with wrapping paper in order to be more decorative with the items.

• If you have an old magazine holder, paint these and cover them with some paper to match the decor, and from there, use them to hold various items, whether it be books, paperwork, or the like.

• If you have old cereal boxes, cover these with wrapping paper, and this will help with divided storage in your desk drawer. Consider using a Stanley knife in order to trim these to your own personal tastes.

Playing and Craft Rooms

The playroom and craft room are pretty good to also work in. Usually, these are chaotic, but with the right steps, and some of these cool ideas, you'll be able to add to this, and make your place even nicer as well.

• For pens and pencils, get a small cup, and put it on the desk in order to hold these.

• For different toys, get some small baskets, separate them by series or type, and then create a cubby system where you can put each of them inside the shelving to make this easier.

• Shoeboxes are great for dolls and doll parts, especially Barbie dolls or some doll clothing.

• For your crafting table, consider using a kitchen island to help with this, since it'll give you more room to work on.

• For leftover ribbon and items, get some old mason jars, and put the items into there.

• Organize all your ribbons based on color in drawers. You can wrap these around cardboard, and from there, you can set the drawers into space for you to hold yourself.

• If you have old magazine racks, you can add them here and use it to store not just your paper, but also your cardstock and craft foam.

• You can sort your buttons in different jars. You can get small little jars for the bigger buttons, and for the smaller ones, you want to use those three-inch spice jars for best results.

• If you have rubber stamps, line them up and stand them up. That way, when you need them, you just take them, and it doesn't affect the space, and it looks pretty cool!

Wardrobe, Closets and Clothes Room

Wardrobes and closets can be hard to organize, but here are a few ways for you to organize these spaces.

• Roll up your clothes and neatly tuck them in. It is great for making sure that you have a lot of space for your items, and it makes the drawers look neat and organized. Rolling clothes helps reduce ironing too!

• Get closet organizers and closet systems to put in place.

• A step stool in your closet will allow you to use the top shelves in the closet, and you'll be able to utilize that space instead of wasting it.

• If you need to use a double hang, do so, since it'll help with horizontal space within the closet.

• Consider over-the-door shoe racks to turn this place into the perfect locale for your accessories or shoes, or both of these things.

• Consider making sure that you keep the items you use the most nearby, and have the ones you don't use as much in different locales.

• Get some small shoeboxes to put the accessories such as different belts, gloves and the like to make it work.

• If needed, get a shoe rack, and use that to help with making sure that you get everything that you need, and to help organize all your shoes.

Storage

• Make sure all of your boxes are properly labeled with the item that they are, and when to use them.

• Make sure that you organize the similar items together, so you're not wasting time.

• Check on this and make sure that you take inventory of the items that you have, so you know exactly what's up there.

• Depending on the space, you should make sure that you have some closed storage containers for items that you'll be putting away like holiday items or seasonal clothing.

• Plastic garment bags should be used for those clothing items that are there.

• Sometimes, if you have wrapping paper, you can get a small little storage container and hold them all in there.

• If you have the space, consider wall-mounted shelves and other furniture items if you don't have that already.

• Always label your items, so you know exactly where it is that you need to go for the items as well.

• If your storage space isn't an attic, consider having some wicker baskets in there and line them up vertically to help with putting different items away.

• Color coordinate containers based on seasons to help with easy access to storage and other items.

• Use clear containers for some of the items that you stockpile that you need to see, such as canned goods, or bulk items that are around and causing trouble.

For most people, clearing out some of the excess clutter in their space is a wonderful way to ensure that you're getting the most out of every inch, to help you with getting the most out of your storage ideas, and out of the storage components that are already there.

CHAPTER 10: TIPS FOR ORGANIZING YOUR STUFF

So how do you organize all your stuff? What are some good ways to organize everything so that it's possible to go through everything and make it easier for you? Well, read below to find out a few of the best organizing tips and tricks to help you with improving your home.

Old Trays and Bowls

While you may use all of your dishes, there are a few ways for you to use them for organization. One great way to organize a crafting or office space is to throw a non-slip mat into a drawer or box to keep them from moving, and then put the bowls in there. Then, put similar items into there. This is a great one if you have a lot of little things, and would prefer to use drawer space rather than jars and such.

Expose It All

If you aren't already exposing everything in your drawers

when you open it, you'll realize that you're only wearing and rewarding the same few things. This can give you a reality of the amount of clothing that you have, and what you're working with. The solution is to fold the clothes in a way that's tight and small, and then store them into the drawers standing up rather than lying flat. That way, you'll see everything right there, and everything is there at a glance. This is kind of similar to how you see the books' spines on a bookshelf, and you'll realize that you either have a lot of clothes you never wear that you can toss, or you'll have a more creative and fun wardrobe that works for you as well.

Like with Like

The worst thing for you to do is to store things that aren't similar to one another, but if you have clothes and household items in multiple spaces, such as the closets, different baskets, or even storage bins, you'll probably forget what you own, and then you over shop for these items. You can from there keep grouped things in one drawer, and all of that is put together. Put items that are similar to one another in a desk, such as stamps, envelopes, pens, and pencils. From there, it's all in one singular location, and it reduces the instance of redundant and boring shopping, and it encourages you to go through and see what you have, weeding out stuff that won't work. When it's all consolidated, it's definitely better for you, and you're saving both money and storage space for items.

Keep Workspaces Clean

If this isn't already done, you need to keep your workspace clean and tidy. The reason for this one is that disorder will impact your long-term success and the fact that you don't have the right idea of where all your stuff is will negatively impact your ability to work and your filing systems. You should understand that our family photos and other small things will draw away our attention all the time. You should do a desk-sweep every now and then, and you should avoid all of the different distractions that are there, and it will help with concentration and focus.

One of the best ways to think about this is to imagine that you have a hotel workspace, and remember, they keep this stuff clean, so make sure that you keep this nice and clean as well.

Streamlining Files

You need to start streamlining your filing system so that all of the paper and documents that you're using aren't sitting there. You should either use a three-tiered filing system, a file drawer for current projects that's close at hand, a second drawer for research material that you need, and then one for documents that are related to the projects that you've done for legal or personal reasons. The third drawer should be considered one that contains valuable documents, and one that you should make sure that you keep on hand for these types of reasons. It's worth considering, and this will help with making sure that you have the simplest and easiest means for this type of experience, and to make it so that you have all of your files on hand.

Try a Shelf Riser

This is a type of shelving that allows you to have double the amount of space in place for storage. This is a good one for those shorter and taller items, and personally, I like using this for a lot of my beauty products. For example, I use jars underneath these, and then the bottles that are up on top. This allows you to have a "spritz and go" sort of lifestyle, and it makes it easier for you to have everything in place that you need for your items.

Another part of this is to tier your shelves too. You will want to make sure that you have the more important items on the bottom, and then the less important ones on top. With this, aim to make sure that you see everything all at once so that if something is amiss, you can get it and then go.

Add a Towel Rack

Towel racks are great because they make organization better. Have you ever thought about adding a towel rack to the closet, such as a linen closet? This is something that a lot of people don't realize is a great one, but it isn't just for bathrooms. Having it over the door creates the out-of-sight storage space for the extra towels, throws, and tablecloths too. This is an excellent way to improve the way your towel rack goes, and it will also help with keeping all of your linens in place too.

Use Color!

If you're not already using colors for organization, you should start to do something about this. This is more than just coordinating your craft ribbons, paper, or clothes. If you're not using it for filing, you're missing out on a lot of the potential benefits that this has. This is great because it helps with adding a few extra ideas to this, and makes it more organized than ever before. Manilla filing folders might work, but if you have a ton of them, one of the best ways to make this work is to use colors for your sorting. For example, you can just glance at the colors and figure out exactly what it is that you need. This will, in turn, help with making sure that you have the right colors to sort everything and anything.

Toiletries on Hooks

Did you know that you can use this with your toiletries? This is pretty great. The best way to do this, however, is to get a second mounted shower curtain, but make sure that it's tension-mounted since it can get heavy. Next, you want to get some clips, such as C slips, and then put them on the shower curtain rail. This is best used close to the wall, opposite of the shower curtain, since it will have to hold a lot of various things. But you can pretty much hang any bottle of something up there that has a plastic tapered end to it. So lotions are great for this, and some body washes come in this form too.

Get Used to Hanging Things

Hanging your items not only looks good, but it also saves you a ton of shelving. We just discussed hanging your toiletries, and we've discussed hanging the office supplies, but one of the best things to hang is pots and pans.

Now, you can do this one of two ways. Either mount these against the wall on the side with some good hooks, or you can get something in the center that contains hooks, hang it up, and then hang them all up here. With this, you should be careful about overloading, but try to hang the bigger pots and pans first, and then work towards the smaller items for best results and the best action possible. That way, you'll have everything neatly in the right place.

For most of us, hanging items is something that we should try to get used to, since this will help immensely with saving your storage space, and making it possible to put just about anything up as well.

Towel Bars Over Sink

Towel bars aren't just for your towels, did you know that you could use this in your kitchen too? This has a similar sort of idea to the hanging idea that we discussed earlier, but a towel bar is great for pretty much any flat surface item. For example, measuring spoons, spices, mugs, or whatever you need, can sit nicely over the sink. The spice racks that they usually sell tend to get expensive, but a towel rack takes all of that out, making it easier, and much better for you to house everything into one specific place, making organizing better, and more possible. This is also good for those of us who are short, since it keeps everything neatly within reach.

Magazine Racks for Tools

We've discussed magazine racks for, of course, files and magazines. But did you know that they can be used for your tools as well for those of us with tool spaces, or crafting spaces that have some hot tools, or even hair products that get hot? You can take them and wind them up around the plug and cord (just be careful to make sure they have cooled down first), and from there, neatly put this in the rack I love this for hairstyling items such as curling irons, flat irons, and the like, and it's super easy and very cheap to use as well.

Get Used to Clear Items

Clear is probably the best color for pretty much any kitchen or personal storage item. That's because, if your kitchen has everything neatly seen, it'll be much easier to look at things. Most people don't realize that their kitchens could be organized better, but having some clear containers let you have a visible look at all of the food and items that you have. It will help with making sure that you have enough space that will work wonders for you, and the clear nature of these is good for you to utilize as well. Consider the clear nature of these canisters, since it'll help with improving the food space as well as quickly seeing what you need to buy.

Use Plastic Shower Pockets

Plastic shower pockets are great not just for shower items, but they're also great for your car! I love using these because they can hold anything that you could need. Most parents are busy, and you should consider this option when storing items. From diaper bags to even small snacks the kids can have, this is a great way to help you with improving your car space, and also makes it easier for going just about anywhere.

But, the cool thing about plastic shower pockets is that they can be used for many different spaces too. For example, crafting items can benefit from this, especially adhesives, and you can also use the hanging parts for a child's lunch or thermos. These are incredibly versatile and waterproof, and it's worth considering if you have a busy schedule, and you need something on the go.

Organization can be hard to begin with, but here, you learned about a few powerful organization tools that'll help with improving your home, and different items with varying uses that are great for you to understand, and use in your space whenever you need to.

CHAPTER 11: DO LESS, LIVE MORE. THE SIMPLE AND MOST EFFECTIVE TO-DOS TO CREATE HABITS AND ROUTINES

Now, the big thing you should also look at is to consider using routines and different to-dos in your home when you're trying to do less and live more. There are a few things that you can use with regards to organization that'll change the game, and we'll discuss them here. They're important to mention, and here, you'll have everything you need on hand to create habits and some routines.

Make a To-Do List

If you're not doing this already, you should have a to-do list for yourself every single day. One of the problems we as humans face is that we're not always certain about what we should be doing next. Or worse, we worry that we're forgetting a very important item that we should've done the day before. And we have a feeling of struggle, hopelessness, and often, those thoughts don't fully go away. This is something that you should also consider if you're looking to keep the thoughts at bay. To do this, you should make a habit of writing down everything, including your short-term and your long-term goals. From there, you should create other to-do lists, separated based on tasks. Listing these out in steps where you need to work towards the goals will help with reclaiming the crisp, results-oriented mindset that you'll use to build and keep the momentum going.

If you finish a to-do, you cross it off. If you have certain days where you clean, then do that. If the goal is to organize the office by the end of the week, each day write down every single item that you need to do.

This might take a long time, but it's a very useful way to get everything that you need done, and it will help keep the momentum going, and keep you nice and strong. To-do lists should become your best friend, especially when organizing, and here, you've seen why most people are benefiting from this, and why they matter.

The "Mis En Place" System

This is a way for a lot of people, and it's more of a professional system that chefs have, but it's a wonderful system that works for many people. It translates to "put in place", which means that you want to gather everything that you need to do an action, such as cook a meal, and from there, clean the work-space and the utensils as you go along.

You can do this with just about anything, from using items for crafting to even cleaning the bathroom. This is very good for keeping hygienic food practices in place too since it reduces the risk of bacteria contaminating foods, and that's something you don't want when you're in the foodservice business. This is a great one for a lot of people to just use in their homes, and it will help you prepare your items faster and more effectively.

Preparing your foods before you cook and clean as you go saves you a lot of time too. If you hate doing the dishes, this is a good way to reduce spending time doing those pesky dishes, and it will help with making cleaning and putting items away much faster as well.

Put It Back Where It Came From

This is something some parents struggle with teaching their kids, but this is a good way to make sure you don't have to spend hours and hours on end cleaning up your home.

The idea is, when you're done using something, you put it back where it came from. Whether it be toys, games, or absolutely anything.

No matter what you use, you put it back where it came from when you're done. This is a way for you to put everything neatly back, and it will help keep you more organized daily. This will better your organization habits, and in turn, will help with improving your wellness, and happiness too. Having this in place will help with improving the daily activities of your space, and it will help you get into the habit of doing this.

I know how hard it can be to do it, but this is one of the best ways to keep your space properly organized and to make your home as versatile and comfortable as it can be.

Leave Items in the Same Spot

This ties into the previous point beforehand, but one of the best ways to get into the habit of making sure that you put it back where it came from, is to leave your keys, wallet, and other items in the same place every single day, and make sure that you have this in an obvious space. Hanging a little key rack in the entryway is a good way to do it. That way, you're never fumbling about wondering whether or not you misplaced these items. It also helps with making sure that you don't tear your entire place apart.

One of the best ways to do this is to get something that will hold the "smalls" as we call them. Entrance tables or a wall-mounted organizer are great for these types of things since they allow for you to store these items easily, and without too much trouble for either of you.

Use a Calendar

If possible, you should try incorporating a calendar into your home. Keep it in a space where you put down some of the different items that you have to go to or major events that you might not be ready for. This helps with an organized life, and you can make a shopping list, some to-dos, some errands, and the like that you need to have on hand.

If you want to have even more of a routine in life, sometimes carrying a small little pocket notebook is good for this. You can incorporate different errands and items you have to do, and some thoughts that might be there. It's very portable, great for users, and it will never need to be recharged like with some of the electronic planners. Upcoming events, notes on things, money spent, things of projects, and the like are great for this, and you can, with this as well, create the best experience that you can, and it's small, but effective for you to have a life that's incredibly organized, and effective as well. It will change the way you get through everything, and it will help with making sure that nothing is left undone.

Have Meal Plans

This is a simple way for people to stay on the ball with not just their home, but also their own body. Your meal plan is one of the easiest ways to stay organized. You can create a daily habit, and from here, update as necessary for you to use. Meal plans also help with creating habits since they allow for you to figure out what you need to make, if you have any items that you need, and cross out items that you don't need. It also puts a good plan of action on the place for you to be, and the time you need to cook these items and any containers that you need to have in place.

Meal plans are one of the simplest ways to ensure that you're getting everything done. Most don't realize it, but meal plans also help keep you on the right track too. You're less tempted to go out for meals, and you won't eat as many bad foods as a result of this. Understanding what it is that you need to make is very important for you to have in place, and in turn, it will help with ensuring that you're on the right track.

Put Together a Routine for Everyone

This isn't just for your kids or yourself, this is for everyone. The routine is everything that they need to do every single day. For kids, this includes laying out the clothes they need to get dressed, their lunches packed and prepared the day before, and where they need to be at what time. You can put together when people need to bathe and shower, and also when you should all be home and any of the events that need to be in place. This also works for chores too, and you should make sure everyone knows the plan and what they need to do for the week. Routines aren't just for you or the other person, but for everyone there, since this will in turn help with improving the way everything works, and the different types of tasks that are there for everyone.

Layout Clothing for the Following Day

This is something that everyone should start to do. Laying this out is the more efficient way of doing this sort of thing. This helps with keeping the critical time during the mornings when you're getting yourself and others ready as well. Laying out clothes the night before makes this easier, and it will save you a bunch of time when figuring this out.

This is something that you should do, not just with yourself, but also with your family, and it will help with this.

You should also make sure that the launch pad area, which is where you go before rushing out the door, is properly put together. You should have a coat rack there for any coats and items, and work bags, school bags, or gym bags, any ingredients for breakfast and lunch, any shoes or umbrellas needed, and anything else that you will want to make sure that you have in place before you begin. Having this routine in place will help keep you on automatic with this, improving your ability to handle everything.

Have an Exact Home for Everything

This final point is a little bit harder, but you should try to have an exact home for everything that you have. That way, when people ask you where something needs to go, you can rattle it off and tell them right away where it needs to go. Spices? Put them on the shelf! Toothbrushes? Have them in a spot under the sink. All of this is great because you'll be the person people will come to when they need to put items away, and it's important to make sure that you have an exact home for them to be in place, and you'll be able to, with all of this, have an exact place, and you'll realize that things are less hectic.

If you don't know where something should go, try to figure out a home for it right then and there. Don't let it sit around because then it'll cause further disorganization, and that's not good for everyone. Having the proper homes in place will ensure that you get everything neatly in its rightful home, and makes it so that you're able to, with the right ideas, create the easiest space to work with, and keep you organized.

Routines make organization better, and a routine allows you to do a whole lot less in life, and lets you do so much more too. If you haven't already put together a small routine or started to put a couple of great routines in place, then you'll want to do it now. The right routines will help with putting it all together, and you can, with these too, live a better, more organized life as a result of this process.

Try it, and you'll see the difference in this right away.

Simple habits and routines change the way you get your organization done, so remember that the next time you feel overwhelmed by the sheer span of your home. If you feel like you need assistance in making your home a simpler place to live, consider all of these tips to help make things easier.

PART 3: CLEAN YOUR HOME IN 15 MINUTES OR LESS

CHAPTER 12: WHAT YOU NEED TO KNOW BEFORE YOU BEGIN

When cleaning your home, there are a few things that make the job easier, and a few things that you should know before you start. It is important to have this mindset in mind before you begin, and in this chapter, we'll tell you what you need to understand before you begin, and why it's important to know exactly what you should before you start. That way, you won't get hung up on all of the stress of cleaning.

Stop Setting Impossible Expectations!

For many who don't clean a lot, they often think they have to have their home so spotless; someone will run their hands over things with a glove that's purely white and will not have a speck of dust on it.

Okay, but if you don't clean a lot, doesn't that seem like excessive effort? People don't realize how stressful that can be for you, and how that can, without actually realizing the impossibility of that expectation, make you feel bad.

People don't realize that setting expectations and goals that aren't realistic won't help. If you only have 15 minutes to clean, you might not get a chance to deep clean one area. Spending an hour deep cleaning one space might be good for a once a month or every few months ordeal, but if you're doing weekly cleaning, you don't have to do that.

When you set up the goals that you need before you clean, you should make sure that it's possible to do. People don't realize that if you set the bar too high or the goal too lofty, you're not going to make it.

When setting these goals, make sure that you understand that while yes, it's wonderful to have high goals that you wish to achieve, also be realistic with the endeavors you wish to achieve with cleaning.

The last thing you want to do is expect to reach for the moon when you're stuck on the ground, and the same goes for cleaning. Don't go into this expecting giant things when you're tackling one area. Don't go in scrubbing it down so hard that your arm cramps. Just clean it, and just be honest with yourself about cleaning. It's a healthier mindset to go into and better for you.

The Number One Enemy: Perfectionism

Perfectionism is probably one of the worst enemies you'll have. That's because perfectionism is something that you should never try to achieve.

If you go into this thinking your home needs to be perfect, you'll fail. It doesn't need to be perfect; it needs to be cleaned.

That means that you clean the space, so it feels welcoming, better, and harmonious. Don't think that you have to just go into this with the idea that you're going to have a clean home, and everything will be okay.

If you're perfect, you'll start to spend way too much time trying to make sure everything is perfect, instead of getting the job done. I know people who obsess over perfectionism, who end up acting like they have to have the perfectly-cleaned home of their dreams. While you should always strive to have a gorgeous home that looks good and feels good, you should also be realistic with your ideas. Make sure that it's clean, but it's also not so clean that you hyper-focus on whether or not everything is perfectly cleaned or not. You should be honest with the way that it looks, and also don't get so hung up on cleaning that it affects you.

Perfectionism is what causes people to spend a bunch of time in one area when they could've just cleaned their whole darn house. It's a nightmare, it's never fun, and you need to be honest about it with the way cleaning is. Be forthright, and make sure that you don't get so focused on being perfect because it'll just make you feel like you're not getting anything done, and it can often make you feel as if you're going crazy every time you try to clean.

The 80/20 Rule

What is that exactly? The concept behind this is to get 80% of your result with only 20% of your effort. This is good because it prevents you from getting hung up on the effort that's put there. You'll definitely do a lot better if you're putting in less effort.

With cleaning, having a plan keeps you focused on the goal.

If you have a set cleaning schedule on who does it, when they do it, when it's time they do the job, and you're not sitting there worried about whether or not the job will get done. You're also not fighting through the concerns of getting it done, and you're not worrying about who is doing what.

It keeps your place less cluttered, and your brain less cluttered.

The best way to get a lot done is with minimal effort. This also involves balancing out everything that's there, and making sure that you're not doing everything all the time. You don't need to wash your windows every single month, nor do you have to clean the gutters every other month unless it's needed. Be flexible, but also be realistic about how you do it.

You should put that 20% of your effort into the places that need it. The kitchen and bathrooms are where the brunt goes, but for rooms and other living spaces, you might need to give them a dusting or two every now and then. You should understand that if you are focusing on the right stuff, you'll be better.

Your showers, toilets, and sinks all get dirtier than say, the bed in the guest room or maybe the pantry if you just use it for food storage. Be smart with where you clean your spaces and don't be afraid to do a little bit less.

Value Your Time

Just like with organizing and decluttering, your time is incredibly valuable. You shouldn't spend all that time trying to clean up one space. If you have one day off, and you're cleaning only for an hour, make it count. Don't get so hung up on the time you spend on something and don't obsess with doing so.

That's something most don't realize. Your time matters more than anything else, and you should always make sure that you work on improving your ability to get the job done. You need to understand that while it might not be perfect, it still is a good job.

That's a big part of cleaning your space. It's making sure you take the time to clean the space in a way that's effective and useful. Be honest with yourself, and with the time that you spend doing this, and if you feel like you're taking far too long on something, then stop doing it. You're not supposed to work on this for so long that you never get anything else done.

Your time is important, and if you're busy already, then you should work on trying to ensure that you use it in all the right spaces.

For some spaces, a yearly clean is fine. When it comes to washing your windows and shutters, do that once a year or so. That's a spring cleaning endeavor. But everything else has its own set time period, and if you know, things will be easier for you.

You need to think of the time you spend cleaning as a finite period. Most people get so hung up on the aspects of cleaning that they don't realize it's only going to kill their drive. You need to, when you start cleaning up spaces, understand that you'll get more done with a plan.

That's why we encourage you to only clean stuff when you have a set schedule and plan, and from there, if you notice that something does have dirt on it, you clean it up. Don't get super into the nitty-gritty of what you need to clean, but just get the job done.

Plans are made for this reason. If you make a plan, you'll be much better off, and you won't get distracted by making sure everything is perfect.

Cleaning is similar to decluttering, since you're taking the time to clean out and take care of a space, and then after it's done, you move onto the next space. Value how your space is handled by looking at each of the areas, and plan accordingly.

CHAPTER 13: THE BEST TOOLS FOR CLEANING!

Now that we've gone over the importance of getting the job done, let's talk about how to clean. What are the best tools for cleaning? What will get the job done quickly and effectively? Read below to find out.

Microfiber Cloths

When you clean a space, microfiber cloths will be your best friend. Lots of people think you need a feather duster or a sponge, but a microfiber cloth will hold on to the dust quickly and easily. Once it's rinsed off, you will be able to use it easily. Plus, the dust doesn't randomly fly away with microfiber cloths.

They're great for cleaning just about anything, from tiles to glass, and it's even good for pet hair off your clothes. One way I like to do it is to have one color to use within the bathrooms, another one for the kitchen, and a third for all of the other areas.

Gone are the days of using those ugly, cumbersome dusters, but instead, you can benefit from this with a simple microfiber cloth. That way, your space is cleaner, and it takes much less time to get the job done.

Vacuums

Vacuums are good for hardwood flooring and of course, carpet. Carpets need this, so a high-quality vacuum will go a long way. I like the kind with a hose on it since you can get it in all of those corners. You can use a hand vac to remove pet hair off the upholstery, freshen up mattresses, and is good for both interior and exterior areas. Even if you don't use a vacuum on a hardwood floor, I encourage you to get one of those stick and hand vacuums.

Stick and hand vacuums also work amazingly in the kitchen since they can get into those little corners far better than a broom and dustpan do. Along with that, there is also the fact that every time you use a broom and dustpan, there's that tiny little line left behind. A vacuum eliminates all of that.

Entrance mats can even be benefitted from with a small vacuum. Once a week, you can give the entrance mat one quick little vacuum over, and it cuts down on the dirt you track inside as well.

This is great if you're someone who wants everything all in one place, and this is indeed how you do that.

Dusting Extensions

If you have high ceilings and you're someone that suffers from indoor allergens, you'll want to get a duster to go up there. But the problem is most people are either too short to reach this or even if they aren't, they need a step stool to get to even the highest chandeliers and light fixtures. Kitchen cupboards do benefit from this too since they are usually too high for the average person. Extension dusters are wonderful, and they offer you a chance to ensure that you have the right length on this, and the perfect dusting experience.

Spray Bottles Along with Homemade Cleaners

Are you tired of having to spend a lot of money on cleaners? Unless you require bleach, you can make spray bottles and fill them up with water, lemon essential oil, and soap to create a nice and beautiful smelling home cleaning product.

You might want to refrain from the essential oil if you have pets, but if you want to make your job easy, you can put the soap and water into a spray bottle, and then use it.

If you want to use spray bottles as well, you can just fill them with water to get the article of clothing ready to be ironed, or even used to train your pets to get away from areas where they don't need to be.

This is a great thing to have, and you can have different cleaners in each of these, and it's wonderful to use if you feel like you're someone that has a lot of cleaning to do, but you don't always want twenty different cleaners.

Scrubbing Sponges

SOS pads and scrubbing sponges are ideal for those tough areas or those areas covered in grease like your oven or sink. These are really tough, they're wiry and take a long time to fully break down, but they are wonderful if you're someone who needs something that gets all of those troublesome areas.

If you have areas with dirt that accumulates, this is how you handle that, since they're ultimately easier to clean if you spend time using these rather than other options that you have. Even just a good scrubbing sponge makes getting grime off the tough locations easier.

Steam Mop

This is a great one to get the grout and the tile cleaned at the same time. If you have washable pads for this, it works too. Shower stalls that are awkward to clean do benefit from this too, and they make sure that the walls are clean. Pretty much almost any surface that's glass can benefit from this, and you can even get some baseboards and facades with this type of cleaner, and it can benefit you immensely as well.

White Cleaning Cloths

White cleaning cloths are probably some of the best for removing any clothing and carpet stains. That's because, colored fabrics will transfer the dyes and from there, expand the problem to make it worse. White cleaning cloths are also super cheap.

These washcloths aren't just good for those who want to clean their home, they're wonderful for removing makeup and other dirt that's there. You can use them to clean up different areas. They can even be used with pet bedding or filling for throw pillows. They're incredibly versatile and they work wonders for you.

Broom and Dustpan

All right, so if you do have hardwood floors, you probably don't want a super huge vacuum. If you're willing to make the job easier for you and get those tough areas that the vacuum can't, such as behind your toilet and the like, then get yourself a broom and dustpan. You can use this along with the vacuum to help clean up everything and make it look better and it's easier for you to do as well. There is a lot that you can do with this, and a lot of amazing benefits that you can do to ensure that you have the right cleaning experience for yourself.

Spin Mop

If you're someone who wants a good mop that's a little more old-fashioned, and you're not really feeling the steam mop or the microfiber mop system, then you should just get a spin mop. These are more of the old-fashioned mop systems, and this one is a spinner that operates with a pedal, so it controls the flow of the water as well. It's very easy to use. On Amazon, there's a ton of wonderful options, and they are good pieces of cleaning equipment.

Wood Cleaner

The problem with some wood finishes is that the wood tends to suffer if there is water applied to it. The solution to that is a wood cleaner. This is good for wooden surfaces and wooden finishes. And it is very easy to use and highly effective as well. Wood cleaners also help eliminate streaks and spots, and they are incredibly useful. These are good for those troublesome kitchen cabinets that tend to have a lot of work added to them, and for those areas that usually require you to use specialty cleaners on them.

Gripping Brush

What, you don't like to use the same sponges for toilets as you would for maybe those troublesome corners? These types of brushes come with that handy little grip added to them that make the job easy, and it also works to make the job a lot of fun. If you're someone that hates dealing with the annoyance of brushes that don't sit right, or maybe you can't reach those corners very well, then you may want to get this one. It also saves you a lot of time on deodorizing and cleaning, as well.

This is good for the kitchen, especially those awkward corners where the drains are, and also those areas that require a little bit more cleaning to them, and it is really helpful for you. They're usually from cleaners with bristled edges, which means they're very easy to use, and they'll get the job done right away.

Stainless Steel Cleaner

Stainless steel cleaners are needed, especially if you have stainless steel items. This is mostly because you will need to clean these in a specific way, but you should consider buying one of these, since it makes the job a little easier on everyone. It reduces the abrasiveness that other cleaners would have, keeping your appliances nice and useful.

And there you have it, all of the tools that you need to ensure that you get the most out of this that you can, and also to help you clean your home readily and easily.

CHAPTER 14: CLEANING TIPS FOR EACH AREA OF THE HOUSE

While you may not clean every area of the house right off the bat, here is a room-by-room guide to cleaning every single area, and what you should minimally do to have a clean space.

While some people might get into the nuances of cleaning, that doesn't mean that you have to be the same way. These are just the minimal options, and it might be beneficial if you're someone that doesn't want to spend copious amounts of time cleaning your stuff.

The Living Room

The living room is your priority, and it's incredibly easy to clean. Below are some of the easy things to do and things that will help with cleaning your living room

• Dust all of the lampshades or use a lint roller to clean them off.

• Use a lint roller to clean off the upholstery too, and make sure the blinds are lightly cleaned off too.

• Wash any of the throws and fluff your pillows as needed.

• Clean off anything that shouldn't be on the sofa with a hand vacuum or using your hands.

• Vacuum the areas under the couches too, since stuff loves to accumulate.

• Polish down your furniture with a wood cleaner.

• Use a microfiber cloth on some of the different electronics there. However, do not use a water-based cleaner but instead, wipe them down.

• Dust any knick knacks with a hand duster or cleaner.

• Always go into this from top to bottom, and make sure that you don't vacuum everything first, but instead, do it at the end.

• Wipe down your ceiling fan since it's simple and prevents all of the dust and other mites from getting around.

• Have your welcome mat shaken outside as needed, so you don't track dust in.

• Fold all blankets and throw them neatly in a basket or corner.

Bedrooms

For the bedroom, it's very simple to clean up too, and there are a few ways for you to clean this up quickly, and effectively.

• For ceiling fans, you can use a duster or sponge to do this easily, or you can get an old pillowcase and clean up your fans and light fixtures, and make sure that when you're done, put them off to the side away from the bed.

• Clean down any mirrors with water and a microfiber cloth.

• Wipe down all surfaces in the area and clean off anything on the nightstands or dressers.

• Take blankets and put them neatly on the bed. If you can, make your bed as well.

• Wipe down your windows with a window cleaner too.

• Use a lint roller again to help clean the curtains, and make sure that you don't track any of that onto any clean bedding.

• Vacuum the floors or sweep them down, making sure to get all corners.

The Kitchen

The kitchen is probably going to be your messiest locale. It's the messiest for most people, but here we'll tell you some of the best ways to clean it down, and some ways to make it easier for you.

• Start at your sink and take care of dirty dishes. Get rid of any dishes that need to be cleaned and put them away as soon as possible. We don't always clean it, but instead, clear it and clean any dirty dishes.

• Wipe down the fridge with a microfiber cloth or even a

scrubbing sponge since it might need it. The curved handle might be helpful here too to get those tight spaces.

• Spray down the surfaces and the stovetop, working from top to bottom, and then, let the cleaner sit. Don't scrub it right away, but instead wait for it to do its thing before you come back.

• Clean down any top surfaces that you can first, and get any of the shelves on top, the light fixtures, and your cabinets too, including the top of the fridge, but do this quickly.

• Clean your microwave and do so by setting a sponge that's wet into there and literally "cook" the sponge for a few minutes. Take a warm rag and dip it in some water and wipe down the doors and sides of the area around the kitchen, or even around the microwave sides. When the sponge is cooled down, wipe both the outside and the inside of the microwave for best results.

• For the stovetop, you should get some baking soda for the stubborn stains. Granite countertops need a specific cleaner and so do stainless steel surfaces, so it's important to make sure that you clean these all down effectively.

• Clean down the vertical surfaces after the horizontal ones, and make sure you get the sides and the handles.

• When you finish, wipe down the sink, and make sure you use an abrasive for the tough stains. When finished, toss the cloth and other items, empty trash, and vacuum or sweep the surface.

Bathroom

The bathroom is going to be your grossest location probably, but it's one of those places that, once it's cleaned up, it looks a lot better. A bathroom that's left unkempt will drive anyone crazy.

• For the shower, you start from the top, and you use a mop to clean it going down or use a scrubbing brush.

• You can also get a grocery bag and fill it with white vinegar, and from there, place it on the showerhead. Remove and rinse.

• Wash your linens and curtains with regular detergent, along with the towels to get rid of mildew on it.

• Clean down any dingy mildew and such with a grout brush and make sure that you get all of the areas since grout is porous, and it does cause bacterial growth.

• For your tiles, make sure that you use an all-purpose cleaner on all of these, and let it sit and mix before you wipe it down.

• Use baking soda on your toilet and make sure that you let it sit for a bit and then brush.

• For bad toilet spots, what you do is get a pumice that's damp and abrasive enough to remove all of the stains that are caused by the mineral deposits on lime, but also gentle enough not to damage the surface.

• Only use an outlet brush after you've worked on getting all of the other stains off of this.

• White vinegar and baking soda poured down your drain and

flushed with hot water will keep all the pipes and drainage nice and clean.

• Use disinfecting wipes to reduce the bacteria in this area since the cloths might transfer the germs from the toilet to the sink.

• Use floss on the faucet, and that's because it gets those grimy spaces between the faucet and your taps as well, and it also cleans the sink easily.

• Finally make sure to de-germ your bathroom vent, and flip it on, remove the cover, and then soak it with a water dish and soap, and from here, wipe it down with a cloth.

• You can also use a paintbrush to get the insides and the nitty-gritty of your bathroom's fan.

• For the floor, either clean it down with a sponge or with a mop and a bucket with hot water.

The Home Office

The home office is probably the one location that you don't spend a lot of time working on, but it's very important to ensure that you have a clean home office too. Here, we'll tell you how to clean down your home office, so it looks spick and span.

• Dust down all the bookshelves, and use a soft-bristle paint-brush to help clean the bindings of books.

• Use an electrostatic dust mop on the storage containers to wipe them down and keep them clean.

• Wipe down your desk surface from top to bottom with a microfiber cloth, picking up anything as you go along the way to dust.

• When cleaning the computer, only use a microfiber cloth, and from there, work from top to bottom, the CPU, and the keyboard with a microfiber cloth, and then use this cloth to wipe down the printer fax machine, and electronics.

• Wipe down the filing cabinets, tables, and other items in your office with a microfiber cloth, from top to bottom. Do all of these but the desk chair.

• For the desk chair, first you vacuum this directly with the brush attachment, and spot treat any of the stains and spills that are seen with a cleaner and cloth.

• Use the cloth to wipe down from top to bottom, and if you notice that the cloth isn't doing enough for it, use a toothbrush, and wipe down the wheels with a toothbrush to scrub necessary spots.

• Disinfect the telephone and remote controls with disinfecting wipes and get all the areas where you use them.

• Use a duster and microfiber cloth to get the light fixtures, and for a fan, wash the fan with a pillowcase to remove the dust.

• Clean your blinds and curtains by using a vacuum on a lower setting with the brush attachment.

• Finally, vacuum everything where you have it, and make sure that you get all of the different areas with the vacuum, moving furniture as needed to clean underneath items.

Craft and Play Rooms

For craft and playrooms, it can get a little chaotic in there. In this, we'll discuss what you should do with all of that stuff in your craft room so you can easily clean it up.

• Go through your supplies, and get rid of any dried paints, primers, mediums, and resins, and make sure that you see if your paints are usable.

• Take all of the crafting items and put them in their spaces.

• Clean up any scrap papers and such. You can use them for other things such as confetti, but if it's not something you need in the immediate future, it's better to toss.

• Wipe down all of the shelves with items, cleaning down any boxes and such with a microfiber cloth.

• If you have a sewing machine, clean it and the foot pedal down with a microfiber cloth.

• For any stains and spots on the floor, scrub them off with a sponge or SOS pad if it's really bad.

• For any toys that aren't put away or any dirty toy sets, get a microfiber cloth and start to wipe all this down.

• When you finish up, you can also sweep the floor, and use a mop whenever you can to ensure that you get the most out of your cleaning experience.

• For crafting projects, make sure the right items are in the right place and wipe down.

• Clean down all shelving too with a microfiber cloth.

• You can vacuum or sweep down the floors if you feel like a vacuum would limit your ability to clean up the space.

Cleaning Your Closets

What they don't tell you is that closets can reek of dust, since it accumulates a lot of dust and grime. Here are some hacks to clean your closets and storage spaces, so they stay nice and clean.

• For closets with actual items in there that you use every day, make sure to take stuff off the top shelf, wipe it down, and then put it back.

• For items that are hanging, go over them with a microfiber cloth.

• Wipe the base of each shelf in a closet since they might get dirty.

• Use a microfiber cloth to wipe down shoes and other items since yes, dust does accumulate on those.

• For any boxes and storage containers, wipe these down as well with a microfiber cloth.

• If you have any grime on the floor, either sweep it, use a mop on it, or a vacuum.

• You can also clean the sides of the hangers with a microfiber cloth, since it will help with cleaning the place down.

• If you're using the organization method where you check to see if you've worn something by turning it around, make sure to check this each time you go into the closet, and if you see unworn stuff, get rid of it.

• Wash any area rugs that you have in there, or any spaces where you leave shoes on since this can attract dirt and grime.

Storage Areas

Storage areas usually don't have to be cleaned all that much, but it depends on whether you go in there a lot. Here, we'll give you a few hacks for cleaning down your storage space, so it looks better and feels nicer.

• Rotate your content here too, so that if something is touched or untouched, you will know, and it's not just sitting there.

• Start with the top, and take inventory of everything that you have in there, and make sure you see stuff that you are using and are organized.

• With a microfiber cloth, you want to go down from the top over each of these areas, and from there, wipe down all the boxes, and excess dirt and other items.

• For boxes that have glitter on it, such as those with Christmas decorations, wipe down all the glitter into a pile.

• Once that's all done, clean any light fixtures there too.

• After that, get a vacuum and also work on cleaning up any of the excess dirt and grime.

With the storage spaces such as your garage, it's usually good to go up and down with a microfiber cloth. As a note too, you don't need to worry about this being a big part of your cleaning routine, unless, of course, you are going to be using the space a lot. But, usually just going through this once every few months is your best bet, since it isn't a space with a lot of usage.

Cleaning your home and storage space is incredibly important, and in this chapter, we discussed how you can do it with each area, in a way that will benefit you, and in a way, where you're getting the job done easily and without too much trouble.

CHAPTER 15: THE 15-MINUTE CLEANING STRATEGY — HOW TO CLEAN YOUR HOME IN JUST 15 MINUTES!

Alright, when we say 15-minute cleaning, we mean a quick, 15-minute cleanup of the home. While this type of cleaning isn't ideal for the tough-to-reach spaces in your home, it's really important for those looking to quickly take care of cleaning since it isn't fun. Here, we'll go over how you can do it, almost as if you're hustling to get the place spruced up for guests as they come over. It might seem like a lot of work, but it's possible, and here, we'll highlight just how you can clean your home in a mere 15 minutes, and the best way to go about doing this.

If you have areas that need a deeper clean, you'll want to make sure that you have a little bit more time for cleaning. But if you don't have the time, or the desire, you want to clean it quickly and want to hit everything in one fell swoop, this is how.

As a note too, the more you clean, the better it is to maintain and the easier it is. So while the first time it might take forever if you keep up with the cleaning schedule, over time you'll do even better, and you'll be happy that you did this. So what are you waiting for? It's time to clean like crazy!

You can do the entire place in one fell swoop, or you can work every single day for 15 minutes to clean a space. We'll tell you how to clean a home with just 15 minutes of work, and how you can set a schedule.

Specific Room Focus

The big thing to remember is to work on the big rooms, which are the bathrooms, the kitchen, and the gathering space. If you're cleaning quickly for company, you can literally just focus on these.

For the living room, you should minimally stash clutter away, work on fluffing and folding blankets, cleaning and vacuuming the floor, and also dusting down anything that has obvious dust on it and wiping down the TV.

For the kitchen, think of the hot items such as the oven and stove, the sink, and the front and sides of the fridge. Wipe these down with a microfiber cloth, or also some cleaner, and from there, wipe down the spaces.

You want to focus on the bathroom but focus primarily on the toilet and sink. Give these a nice wipe down, and from there, also consider what the shower looks like too. If you're pressed for time, you don't clean it. You should as well look at cleaning the kitchen and the den, and sweeping it down, rather than vacuuming it cause that takes a little bit more time and more equipment.

The focus should be to wipe down the surfaces that you have, and make sure that they are nicely cleaned off. You should also have dust cloths to get rid of the dust that's there, and it would best be used in areas where people may not know. The same goes for disinfectant wipes so that you can wipe these down on surfaces of the bathroom, and of course, on the kitchen counter.

But what if you're someone who wants a more standard cleaning schedule, where you don't have to hustle and put everything away in just 15 minutes? Wouldn't this be easier? Of course, it is! You can do it, and here, we'll tell you how to put together the simple cleaning schedule that will help you.

The 15 Minutes a Day Cleaning Schedule

This type of schedule focuses less on just preparing the home and hoping to so that nobody sees any faults, and more on doing a little bit each day. While yes, you might notice that you have a messy bathroom or bedroom, you can use this type of schedule to help you get the most out of this.

How do you do it? Well, we'll tell you each day what you should do and what will be best. This is a good strategy to employ, however, after you've done the cleaning already and want to maintain it. This is better for maintenance rather than going down and cleaning everything.

For Monday, you vacuum, and you vacuum the entire house completely. Vacuum the rooms, sometimes do your vents and curtains and the crevices of windows. If your home is really big, it might take a little more time, but 15 minutes should suffice. Some people use a robot vacuum to get all the surfaces clean for an easier time. If you want to do it another way, literally sweep down the hardwood surfaces, and then vacuum at the end if you have hardwood floors throughout your house.

Tuesday is dust day, and this should take about 15 minutes, but this also depends on the knick knacks you have. You may need to wipe down the furniture as well with the furniture polish that you have too.

On Wednesdays, you have the bathroom. This might be your only bathroom, or it could be your main bathroom. But what you want to do is you should clean down the toilet, the counters, the mirror, the tub, the shower, and of course, your floors. In general, the total time for the bathroom should be around 15 minutes or so.

On Thursdays, you can do this again, or alternatively, if you don't have another bathroom, but you have a playroom and craft room, you clean these down, simply by picking up some of the items that you have and making sure everything is kept nice and tidy. This again should only take 15 minutes, and usually, it's just cleaning anything extra that you have on the ground.

The kitchen is what you do on Fridays, where you clean down the countertops and surfaces with the product, and you also wipe down the fridge and the tops of surfaces. This is something that again, should take you no more than about 15 minutes.

Now Sunday, you have two options. Either you don't do a darn thing, or you do small projects. That again is dependent on how your home is looking. If you have cleaning projects you've been holding off doing, such as the storage rooms and your closets, you do them at this time. This is something simple and yet very effective.

When you look at this, you might wonder if I'm joking or something. After all, it's super simple, right? Well that's the thing, it doesn't need to be some in-depth cleaning once you have it clean. People think cleaning should only be done when it's dirty, but that really isn't the case.

Cleaning is done when it is scheduled to be done, or if there is a mess that should be picked up right away. The idea behind it is if you do clean this, you immediately get it out of your life, out of your hair, and it's all taken care of. You should put all the mail away in a basket, and sort out the mail for anything that comes in. Throw out all junk, and from there, make sure that everything is picked up.

This might seem very simple to the average person. But, here's the thing, with this type of system, it's a maintaining step. You're not working towards perfections.

While in the last chapter we gave some awesome cleaning hacks, you've got to understand that it's not necessary to do it like this. Not at all. In fact, I don't recommend you do it all like this, but instead, you should wipe it all down. You need to look at the space and envision how you want to do this.

You have to work from top to bottom as well. It saves you time and effort when cleaning up the different spaces, and it's pretty easy.

Skipping?

This is something I honestly only recommend if you are desperate and don't have time for it. For those parents who are expecting, who have appointments, or those dealing with potty training, a kid crying all day, or whatever, you should skip it only if it's unable to be done. While it won't hurt your house if it isn't done in a specific week, you don't want to create a habit. This does make a difference though, especially if you look at it this way.

The idea behind the 15 minutes of cleaning a day isn't to force you to have to do it like it's a chore, even though it technically is a chore, it's important to realize that if you treat it like this, it takes far less time, and far less effort to get it done. It makes it so simple, and also very effective for you too. It's a fun way for you to easily create and clean your home, offering you the best and simplest experience for you to attain.

Cleaning your home in just 15 minutes a day is utterly possible and doable, and you'll realize that, once it's all taken care of, and you've fully cleaned it, you'll be happier than ever before, and you'll be able to attain it all.

PART 4: HAVE FUN!

CHAPTER 16: HOW TO GET THE FAMILY TO WORK TOGETHER

You will need assistance with this one. That's because getting your family to clean isn't always the easiest thing, but it is completely possible. In this chapter, we'll discuss how to get everyone involved in cleaning and how you can do it too.

Do or Delegate — How This Gets Everyone to Cooperate

This is a concept that's important to utilize when you're trying to get everyone to work together.

The idea is that either you say you're going to do it, or you delegate it to other people. This can be anything from washing the dishes to even dusting the knick knacks on the shelf. You either do this, or you delegate the task to others.

There is power in numbers, and there's a lot of benefits to be had if you spend time giving other people different tasks rather than doing it yourself. For example, do you want to spend all your time vacuuming all the floors and areas, or would you rather delegate it to another person in the house?

The general idea you should follow is that if it's something that can be done by someone to a satisfactory result, then you should delegate it. If you know the other person won't screw it up, then you should delegate it.

If it's a specialized task, then you should do it. That's because you're kind of the "expert" in that case, which means that you're the one who knows what to do in this case, and you should make sure that you do the job how you want it to be done.

But, if you think you can easily get the same results from someone else, delegate it.

There's a concept in making lives less stressful in the office, where you should try to delegate at least 2/3 of the tasks to others. While some stuff is usually best done by yourself, for these chores, if you get others involved, it saves you so much time.

For example, if you spend an hour cleaning every day, and you've got 4 people in the house, have them each take a quarter of the work. That brings your cleaning down to 15 minutes.

Everyone can get involved in this. And the best way to do this is to sit down with everyone in the home and get an agreement between all parties on what it is that you need done, and what they're willing to help you with. If you know what that is then you'll be good to go.

Delegating tasks is so important for people who are looking to get the most that they can out of the time that they spend cleaning. You can save yourself so much time if you do this, and it saves a ton of headaches and hardships, so if you can, always work to delegate all the tasks at hand, and make it so that you're able to, without fail, make the job of cleaning your home and making the space more functional for everyone.

You can start using this today by going through a list of the tasks at hand, and rattle off who does what. You'll then have everyone on the same page of what exactly needs to be done, saving you a lot of headaches and annoyance too.

How to Get Kids Involved in Cleaning

For many parents, this can be the hardest step. Children are incredibly helpful with cleaning and decluttering the home, but there are two concerns most parents have when they try to get their kids to help.

The first of these is what they can do. What can children do in this case? It does ultimately depend on what their capabilities are, but children are great for cleaning assistance. You'll be amazed by the results this will get, and the fun that's there.

Now some chores are better for kids than others. For example, if you're looking to get younger kids involved, maybe have them get used to putting their toys away, making their bed, or picking their stuffed animals up off the floor.

Slightly older kids can help with dusting some areas, or even just using the sponge on surfaces that are closer to their height to help get the lower areas.

Some older kids can handle more involved chores. For example, if you have vacuuming, sweeping, or even doing laundry, they can help with that and make the job easier.

However, do be fair to your kids. Give them a chore list of things they should do. Don't force them to clean the whole house like some parents, but instead, be fair with it. Give the same amount of chores to each of the kids, and get incentives in place to make them do this. For example, if you know they like an allowance, give them an allowance each week for doing the job. If they do the chores for X amount of weeks, they can get some ice cream or another treat. It's a wonderful way to get everybody involved, and it's a fun way to make the job even better and more doable for everybody that's doing it.

For a lot of people, there are a lot of benefits to be had from this, so definitely consider all of these different things kids can do so that they can help with the chores. You should make sure they're doing stuff that's within the age range and provide reasons and incentives for doing things too.

Treat This Like a Game!

It is a game in a sense, and it's important to realize that if you treat it like this, you'll be much happier off. Cleaning isn't fun, decluttering isn't fun, and organizing can be so boring, but sometimes, treating this like a game is something that most people end up doing. If you do end up treating stuff as a game, you'll be so much happier.

For example, try treating putting away dishes as a race to see how quickly you can get it done. For children, you could say that the one who puts their toys away the fastest gets an extra treat, or maybe they get to choose the next movie for family movie night. You can even make a game up where an evil monster is going to come in 15 minutes, and they need to put their toys away and clean up the bedroom fast! You can even tell them as well that they're competing against their siblings to see who will get the job done quickest.

No matter what you do, where you go with this, and how you do it, you should try making a game out of it.

Games help get kids excited. It's a little less like cleaning and a little more like a fun game that can certainly make things easier. If you notice that your children aren't all that interested in doing this, it can give them a reason to. A lot of people don't realize how helpful a game can be with this, since it can ultimately make it possible for you to deal with a lot of the chores easier.

If you notice your kids are reluctant to clean up, then you should consider potentially doing this, since it gets everyone on the right track, and helps push forth new games to keep them stimulated, since kids will love it if there is a possible game in the fray here.

Games are fun, and they're good for kids, since they can make dealing with the job a lot better.

Races are usually the best kinds of games in this sense since most people who do races tend to get the kids to all work together. They can do races against the other siblings, or even against the whole house. All while making it a decent experience for them too.

Lots of parents get a lot of great benefits from this, and you should consider this type of thing if you want your kids to all work together, and to make it easier for everyone as well.

For some parents as well, making it a game makes it easier for them. It keeps them motivated, and it can be a way to try and better this type of experience too. For most parents, it can make things easier for them to accomplish the tasks, and even those who aren't parents and are just trying to make their home nicer, it can improve on this markedly.

There are many different ways to make cleaning possible, and I encourage you to get everybody involved. That way, people are contributing to the household, so you're not doing everything, and you also end up with a cleaner, better home than ever before.

CHAPTER 17: HOW TO STAY MOTIVATED

Let's face it: cleaning is super boring, and not always the most fun thing. If you have a big home, this is even harder to accomplish. You need to learn how to stay motivated, though, to get more done and to feel happy.

For larger spaces, this is very important, especially since it can take a long time. If you have hoarder tendencies, this is a great way to get the job done, and you'll be really happy with the efforts over time.

Staying motivated, however, can be a struggle, because it can be a lot of work. Most people don't realize how annoying it can be. But, in this chapter, we'll give you some good motivational tips to keep in mind, and efforts to apply so that you can stay on track, and stay happy with the results that you get from this. Most don't realize how important this is, and how things will change with the right motivation and the right ideas to have.

You Need That Motivation, So Stay Inspired!

Motivation comes in so many forms. Whether it be the idea of a fully organized home, having something that looks like something out of a Better Homes and Gardens catalog, or whatever, having the correct motivation is something we all can benefit from.

Motivation is something you can use even in the worst of times, in the harshest of moments, and it can change the way you do things.

Most people don't even realize that this is so important for the majority of us, and it's something that a lot don't realize will help us get through the worst to get the job done.

For example, if you know the best motivation for yourself is you will be able to spend less time looking for items, then this might be a good thing for you.

If you know your motivation is to have less clutter on the floor, then use that as your drive. If you have a dream home that you'd love to emulate, but it requires you to clean up the space, then do that. The biggest thing to remember is whatever you choose, you need to have the motivation in place.

With anything in life, motivation is the reason why stuff gets done. It's the reason why you get what you want, and why things work so well for you. If you don't have that, you can say goodbye to getting the job done.

And one way to also do this is to make a goals list. You can write down both the main goals and sub-goals that you will want to keep in mind. You can even make a timetable of all the different stuff you want to get done, and how long it will take to do all this. That way, you'll have an idea of what exactly it is that you need to do to achieve the results that you want.

What most don't realize is that if you have goals and you have a game plan, you'll have a great time. That's because, if you have a set idea of how you want to achieve everything, you can always come back to this.

Sometimes, even keeping motivational quotes around to look at every so often helps too. While it might seem weird to do this for cleaning a house, it's useful and helpful, and it will be beneficial for you as well when you need that extra bit of motivation.

Sometimes, if you talk to other people who are doing similar things, it helps a lot. Maybe you can talk to other friends or even family members, and all of you make a game out of this. The person who cleans their house up the best and the fastest wins. This can be great for some people, and it can give you a reason to do it, even on those days that you don't want to.

You can also try the motivation of big parties. Having a big party, for example at a certain time, will help you stay motivated too since this big party can account for a lot of the different parts of life, and also account for all the things you want to have accomplished. If you do have a big party set for a certain period of time, you can clean up the house, and from there, try to declutter and organize your space, and from there when it's time for guests to arrive, you're not shoving stuff in the closet, but instead, you're showing everyone your wonderful, beautiful abode.

Whatever your reason is or isn't, have some motivation there, and it's very important to understand that the right motivation will help immensely. It will change the way you handle life and the way things go. By having the correct motivation in place, you'll be much better off, and it can help you with improving your wellness too.

How You Can Stay Inspired

How do you stay inspired in the face of so much work? How do you stay positive throughout all this?

Well, there's a lot that you can do to accomplish this. For example, you need to sit down and think about what inspires you. Is it the idea that you'll be able to find everything quickly and effectively? Or is it the fact that you also have a plan that works and makes sense for you to do? Whatever it is, you should look at the inspiration you want to have, and what will get you excited and happy.

It doesn't have to be something huge. It can be something small, but that little nugget of inspiration will keep you nice and on track, and you'll be ready to make it work.

I personally like to look at different areas for inspiration. Some of the different areas where you'll feel inspired include the following:

• Magazines

• Other people's homes and spaces

• The different pictures online

• Brainstorm ideas on how having a clean space inspires you

• Different benefits of having a clean home, and how it can benefit you.

All of these different ways will help you improve your home and the space that you have. What many of us don't realize is that if we don't take the time to look for the inspiration that we want to have when you get the job done, it can make decluttering almost like a chore.

Sometimes, also looking at just how far you've come will help too. I remember when I started to clean my space, I felt a bit bogged down by the way things were going. I started to, with the cleaning that I did, imagine all of the progress that was happening in my space, and everything that was going on. I started to look at that, and I started to realize that I did so much already, and I can continue for the long haul if needed.

Even just looking at this will help you stay positive and inspired. Most don't even realize how important this can be, and how just a little bit of inspiration can change your life, but it does. It really can mean a difference in the long haul, and it can make your life better and easier.

So yes, look for inspiration, look for all of the different ways you can better your home, and some of the different ways to organize yourself, and from there, you'll be able to change all of this and change your entire life for the positive.

Do this, and you'll see the difference that it makes not only in the current situation of how your space looks, but also, in the way your space looks later on.

Celebrating a New Home, a New Life

It goes without saying that once you've cleaned up your home, it will change your life. In most cases, you'll start to notice that the second you start putting everything together. You'll realize that it's easier to live life. The ease of life will make you happy, and it will make you feel good.

For most people, having the ease in place does make things a little bit better, as well. It'll allow for you to look at your space and see the truth of it, that it looks and feels better too.

Clean homes make you feel accomplished. Even if you do a little bit, it goes a long way.

If you clean up your home, take pictures along the way too. This is a great way to make sure that you have the evidence of change. Whenever you feel down, pull out these photos. You'll see the difference, and how for you've come. Even over the year, if your project is a big one, you'll see the changes that you want to make. You'll be amazed at how different it can be for you, and how everything changes.

When you're cleaning your home, you will notice that when it comes to the process of cleaning it, it isn't fun, but it will help you see the potential that you've made so far. You can get a good feel for how far you've come, and how much you've accomplished by taking pictures and reporting progress.

The idea of seeing how far you've come in a clean home is a

great way to inspire others to clean, and also will help you feel proud of the progress you've accomplished. For most people, they'll be able to feel inspired to get further with their progress. And it will help them to get a much better result from their activities, and build a better and cleaner home.

Start doing this today, figure out your motivation today, and you won't regret anything that you do.

CONCLUSION

Decluttering, cleaning, and organizing your home is most definitely possible. You have to go through the different steps to do it.

For those who are interested in decluttering, you learned everything that you need to know to declutter your home, from how to start handling all of the junk that you have. You also learned about the three piles, how they apply to the clutter you have lying about, and how you can, with just decluttering, have a much less messy space.

There is also the aspect of decluttering where you feel the sentiment for the items that you have. You'll realize as well that the sentimental feelings that you have for those items are just your brain trying to rationalize holding onto these things, and you'll realize as well that, once you start to clean up the space, you'll have a much happier, and healthier mindset too.

Organizing is something most people hate to do, simply because it takes a lot of effort to do, and you feel like you have to organize to the standard of one of those Good House-keeping catalogs. But you don't. There are simple ways to make sure your space stays organized, and here, you've learned some of the optimal ways to make sure that you have the best organization possible, and you'll be able to, with this as well, understand that there are a lot of benefits to be had with this, and a lot that you can do with it.

For so many people, cleaning is the hardest part of this. Who likes cleaning anyways? Well, you don't have to suffer from the travails of cleaning anymore, and you'll be able to, with this book, have all the cleaning tools that you need, and you'll learn all of the quick and dirty ways to clean your stuff and maintain a happy space.

You'll be able to make sure that you get everyone nice and motivated as well. You should have fun with this, and we talked about how you can have a lot of fun with cleaning, and the best ways to ensure that you're cleaning and making an effort to bring forth some wonderful and amazing spaces that you'll feel proud of.

No longer do you have to spend your time setting down your items and forgetting them. You'll form habits that are invaluable and are fun to achieve. You'll realize that by doing this, you build a much healthier mindset, and you'll get your house cleaned up in no time. What many don't realize is how important it is to put this in place, and how, by just implementing all of these changes, you'll make a difference in no time.

Stop setting and forgetting it. Stop thinking that you have only a few minutes to do things and therefore you can't do anything about it. Instead, start to form different habitual activities that'll benefit you, and start to put forth a better, more rewarding process to help you ensure that you get the most out of this. Start to put together habits, and start cleaning and organizing your home, along with decluttering all of those troublesome spaces, today. You'll be grateful for this.

REFERENCES

Mique. (8 Feb. 2017). *Simple 15 minute a day cleaning schedule.* Retrieved from: https://www.thirtyhandmadedays.com/15-minute-day-cleaning-schedule/

10 Cleaning tools Everyone Should Own. Retrieved from: https://housewifehowtos.com/clean/10-cleaning-tools-everyone-should-own/

(27 Apr. 2018). Organize Your Storage Room with These 18 Decluttering Ideas. Retrieved from:

https://www.extraspace.com/blog/home-organization/room-organization/storage-room-organization-ideas-tips-to-declutter/

Jenn. *How to Declutter and Organize Any Space.* Retrieved from: https://www.cleanandscentsible.com/how-to-declutter-and-organize-any-space/

Michel, B. T*he Stupid Simple Solution to Declutter Your Home and Keep It that Way.* Retrieved from: https://www.familyfelicity.com/simple-steps-declutter-home/

Babauta, L. *18 five-minute Decluttering Tips to Start Conquering Your Mess.* Retrieved from: https://zenhabits.net/18-five-minute-decluttering-tips-to-start-conquering-your-mess/

Amy. *Decluttering Paralysis: Strategies When you're Struggling to Declutter.* Retrieved from: https://organizationboutique.com/decluttering-paralysis/

Kaplan, J. (3 Nov. 2019). *7 Reasons to Declutter Rooms.* Retrieved from: https://www.thespruce.com/reasons-to-declutter-right-now-4140438

Ongaro, A. *5 Ways to Start Decluttering Today!).* Retrieved from: https://www.breakthetwitch.com/start-decluttering/

How to Organize Storage Rooms. Retrieved from: https://homeguides.sfgate.com/organize-storage-rooms-54201.html

Baginski, K. and Miller, M. (27 Feb. 2019). *15 Quick Tips for Keeping an Organized Kitchen.* Retrieved from: https://www.hgtv.com/design/rooms/kitchens/quick-tips-for-keeping-an-organized-kitchen-pictures

Pinksky, S. T*he Ultimate Room-By-Room Organization Guide.* Retrieved from: https://www.addititudemag.com/slideshows/how-to-organize-your-home-room-by-room/

Nystul, J. (24 Jun. 2014). *A Step-by-Step Guide to a Clean Kitchen.* Retrieved from: https://www.onegoodthingbyjillee.com/step-step-clean-kitchen/

Milton Keynes UK
Ingram Content Group UK Ltd.
UKHW011340030324
438845UK00002B/453